Wonderful

Old

Women

outskirts
press

Outskirts Press, Inc.
http://www.outskirtspress.com

ISBN: 978-1-4787-8314-5

Outskirts Press and the "OP" logo are trademarks belonging to Outskirts Press, Inc.

PRINTED IN THE UNITED STATES OF AMERICA

I dedicate this book to the thirteen wonderful women we interviewed and photographed and to three other women who made the book happen-- Deb Field, Linda Harris, and Margaret Pomeroy.

Bonnie

TABLE OF CONTENTS

INTRODUCTION

Why women and why women over 80? Consider this common insult: "You drive like a little old lady." This cliché suggests old women are all alike and all are negligible and negative—limited, timid, hesitant, implicitly uninteresting and unimportant. Ageism and sexism embodied in three words. Well, all women, if we are lucky, will become old women—the only other option is death. All of us know that we live in a youth culture in which nothing is considered more flattering than to be told you don't look your age. Poor Blanche Dubois hiding from natural light and lying about her age—at 30, no less. At my own seventy-first birthday celebration, the server grinned as she asked if I was 29.

Our culture provides us with numerous models of wise old men, historical and literary: Einstein, Mandela, the Dali Lama, Tiresias, the Ancient Mariner. But where are our paradigmatic or archetypal wise old women? Historical and cultural models are hard to find. But, in truth, if we look around us, really look with clear eyes and open hearts, we see them. They were there all the time—simply not seen because our eyes did not focus on them. Just as literature and history change when the focus is on ordinary people, or minorities, or women instead of military battles and wars and treaties, so when we focus on old women and not young women, we see newly. Many of us, maybe most of us, fear aging. Since the culture values women for our youth and beauty, we women often fear aging more than men do. In our culture where men are valued for their power, and money is the bottom line, a rich old man still has "cultural capital."

All of us need examples of women who are elders, who have not spent their lives denying their age. We need women who have lived deeply, who see life as an on-going process, and who recognize themselves as ever-changing. In these interviews you will encounter a few of those wise women. Some of them have significant achievements in their fields, but **all** have lived intensely and continue to have interesting, evolving lives.

How did Deb and I pick these particular women? We began with friends and neighbors— women we already knew and admired, and in some cases, loved. In interviewing them we were celebrating them and offering portraits of women who have helped us grow. After that, we reached out to other people in the community, to friends of friends, for suggestions, women other women and men admired—and made new friends along the way.

This is not a collection of interviews with a *thesis* or single story line. Each woman and story is unique. We certainly are not saying that all women over 80 are marvelous. They aren't, any more than all people of any group are. We are simply introducing you to a few marvelous, old women. We have aimed for a wide variety of background and experience and consciously avoided already celebrated women. Economically they range from modest to wealthy. Our interview subjects are Protestant, Catholic, Jewish, Muslim, unaffiliated; they are white, black, Mexican-American, Puerto Rican-American, Iraqi-American. All of these women—age 80 to 97—currently live in San Antonio, but almost all were born and lived in other parts of the country and world at some stage of their lives.

Although the interviews are intentionally personal, historical events (World War II, the Holocaust, the Korean War, 9/11) and cultural and social problems (racism, anti-Semitism, sexism) are often crucial parts of their lives and stories. How each experienced and responded to limitations, difficulties, losses, and pain is central to her character and her story.

We encouraged each woman to tell her own story in her own way: how she currently saw herself and her life-journey. All of us tell our stories in different ways; what you read here is how each woman saw herself at one point of her life. That she might have seen herself differently ten years ago or may look at things differently five years from now is proof of the fluidity of both life and memory.

What about our interview process? We listened and recorded each interview; Deb transcribed them and did the first editing; then I edited an initial draft and sent it to the woman herself to correct and change. Some of the women wanted their colorful language changed into more correct, standard English. Some had second thoughts about vivid comments they had made about their own feelings, family members, or friends. In every case we (sometimes reluctantly) followed their wishes. Each woman got the chance to decide how she wanted to *present* herself, including second thoughts!

It has been a bumpy, exhilarating process for all of us—interview subjects, Deb, Linda (our photographer) and me. Obviously Deb and I couldn't ask other women to look at themselves and their lives without, at least unconsciously, asking ourselves what we would say if interviewed.

We hope this book will be a source of joy and pride to the interview subjects, and that after reading these interviews, readers will also have less dread of aging, more sense of continuing possible growth in their own lives and awareness, and a vision of becoming wise old women (or men) themselves.

A salute to our worthy elders, Wonderful Old Women!

Bonnie Lyons

Transplanted New Yorker, Maxine Smolins worked for decades as a psychiatric social worker and social activist with the ACLU. Her bone-deep optimism helped her work successfully for decades with abused children. Although she has experienced many physical problems (beginning with a serious car wreck on her honeymoon) and diseases over the years, her resilience, humor, and love of life totally dominate her outlook, so absolutely no one can believe she is 91.

MAXINE SMOLINS

M: Tell me about this project you're beginning.

Our culture has the idea about the wise old man but no wise old women, just the old witch or the woman in the shoe who didn't know what to do. Deb and I KNOW there are wise old women and we want others, especially young women, to hear your stories.

M: That's lovely-- now go find one.

We consider you one!

M: I'm 90 but I don't consider myself wise. Just lucky.

There you go! You never take any credit! Let's start with family history. Were your parents immigrants?

M: Yes. The "legendary" figure in my family was my mother's mother. She was the daughter of a poor rabbi in Russia. The family married her off thinking it was a good thing to do, but she didn't love him. After she married him, she came back to her family and said, "I can't do this. I want a divorce," which was unheard of at that time. But she was insistent. Her husband would not give her a divorce and she said, "Well, I'm not living with him," so she went to work at a cigarette factory and learned how to roll cigarettes. She was promoted several times. A couple of years passed and she kept insisting she wanted a divorce, but her husband wouldn't agree and thought he could wear her down. Then she met my grandfather who was a musician and a wonderful man. My grandmother adored him and he was the love of her life. Finally her husband gave her a divorce; my grandparents married and she was happy.

Was your mother born in Russia?

M: No. In Russia at that time Jewish men were sent to the military at a young age and never got out. My grandmother saw that and said, "We have to leave." So my grandparents snuck out of Russia with no papers and little money. Just the two of them and they traveled through various countries in Europe and ended up in France. She was the brains of the outfit; he was the musician, the heart. She found an area in Paris where the Jews lived and she said, "This is where we can live." My grandmother spoke Yiddish and learned to speak French. My grandfather was a musician; however, he didn't have his papers so he couldn't get into the musicians' union and earn a living as a musician. He ended up being a peddler, and that wasn't very lucrative. My grandmother rolled cigarettes for the White Russians who came to Paris. This was on the QT, because you weren't supposed to do this. My mother told me she remembered my grandmother sitting with a board on her lap rolling cigarettes. My grandfather would deliver them to the Russians. It didn't take long for them to realize that this wasn't enough to live on. At that time there were many men in Paris who had mistresses; they would set up house for them and needed furnishings. My grandfather bought pawned furniture and they set up a small second hand furniture shop on a busy corner that my grandmother had noticed. My mother said she remembered her mother putting up mirrors on the walls to make the shop look bigger and look like there was more to choose from. The family lived above the shop and that's where my mother and her brothers grew up. But then came the Dreyfus case. Paris streets were ablaze with anti–Semitism, and one morning my grandparents came down to the store and written on the windows was "Dirty Jew" in French. It frightened my grandmother and she said, "This is like Russia and we have to leave!" So, again, they fled and this time they came to America.

How old was your mother when they arrived in the US?

M: My mother was 12 and her mother was maybe 50. They ended up in New York on the Lower East Side because they could speak Yiddish and everyone on the Lower East Side did too. When my mother went to school, the teachers called her "the little French girl" and she got special treatment—the snobs. Ultimately my grandfather was able to become a musician here in the States. He didn't do big things; he played at bar mitzvahs and weddings. He played the cornet. They never made a lot of money but they managed. So that's their story.

Were you brought up speaking French and Yiddish?

M: I was not. I know a little Yiddish, which I learned from that grandmother. When my older brother was born, my mother spoke to him in French. She thought that would be helpful. But when he went to school and spoke French, the kids made fun of him. My father was furious. He said, "How can we live in this country and our children don't speak English? Do not speak to our children in French." So, I didn't learn French.

What was your father's background?

M: My father was born in Warsaw, which was under Polish and Russian rule in those years. He was very bright, and at that time the laws were that Jewish children couldn't go beyond elementary school. His family recognized he was bright and decided to leave. Where did they go? In their infinite wisdom--to Germany, the intellectual capital of the world. My father got his education there. Then his mother, whom he adored, died. When my father's father married again, my father couldn't accept his stepmother so he left Germany. First he went to Belgium where there was family and later he went to England where he also had family. At that time everyone took in relatives. When he decided to come to America he was in his late 20s. My dad was a linguist, he spoke five languages. He got a job with an import/export company because of his knowledge of languages. He traveled back and forth to Europe. He met my mother through a friend. I wish I could say it was a happy marriage. It was not. They were both wonderful people but there were problems. My mother had two sons very close together and she didn't want any more children. But then she got pregnant with me. What saved the situation was that I was a girl and that was a novelty for her. I was born in May and her beloved father had just died in April. I was named after him. His name was Max and they named me Maxine. I had all this luck. She received me with a great deal of love because I was a girl and her father's namesake.

Did your father's family ever come to America?

M: They were still in Germany and many of them did not survive the Holocaust. My dad was always busy sending money and packages to those who survived. One of the reasons my father came to this country was because of his belief in social justice. He had a big picture of Abraham Lincoln over his desk. He named my brother Julian Lincoln Glass. He was a real social justice person. He believed this country was wonderful. He and my oldest brother used to have lots of discussions. My brother would say, "Dad, you don't see this or that" and my dad would say, "This is the best country, and if you don't see that, you are a fool." At our dinner table that's all that was discussed: politics. Ironically, these were people who had no power. On Sunday my uncle and an aunt would come over and they'd sit around the table and say Roosevelt should do this or that and be critical of what was going on; they all had opinions. I grew up in that kind of house. My brother used to stand on the corner and make speeches against war and fascism!

How has that affected you, Maxine?

M: I've always been involved in politics and I still am. I'm active in the ACLU and the Democratic Party. My husband, Sol, was also ardent for social justice and my daughters and I are all social workers. It's still part of the bread and butter of the home.

You always talk about yourself as lucky. Why do you never give yourself credit?

M: Because it's true! So much of my life has been luck. Just wonderful good luck. To be healthy, to have good genes, to come from wonderful people. I listen to the news and hear about poor immigrants on boats who can't find a place to land. Talk about luck. It's overwhelming. I can't say enough about that. It defines who I am. I got the richness of so much; I'm very grateful and I'm very lucky.

I'm amazed that you describe yourself as healthy. You've had so many health problems.

M: I've had cancer twice but I was lucky. It was caught in time. People die. I didn't.

I remember when you got it. Deb, listen to this story. Maxine and I are in a book group together and at one holiday dinner and I said," Maxine how are you?" and she said, "I was diagnosed with breast cancer today. I thought I'd stay home and cry but what good would that do. So I came." Tell us about the second bout of cancer.

M: I had lung cancer and a lobe removed. I was lucky. We all know women who have died. And I have macular degeneration and get an injection in my eye once a month. But it works! I broke both femurs a few years ago and spent months in rehab, but things have worked out well. You know, my mother was a very positive person and an important influence on me. She was a happy person and sang opera while she cleaned the house. She'd go around the house dusting and singing La Boheme. Can you imagine? She kept a neat house but didn't let chores dominate her. She had this great saying: my dishes are my friends. They always wait for me! She was a wonderful woman and she adored me.

What was your relationship with your brothers like?

M: Very fine with both. My older brother, who was seven years older than I, was very good to me. He introduced me to my husband, Sol. He was a caretaker and a really nice guy. He went to Brooklyn College where he got a masters degree in economics. Smart as hell. When I had trouble with math in school, he sat with me and taught me algebra and looked after me. He was wonderful to me. When he graduated, he applied to Macy's. On the application they had a box for religion and he wrote Jewish. They interviewed him and told him they liked him very much but weren't sure about hiring a Jewish person. It was a strike against him. Can you imagine that they would say that overtly? That was the time, though.

When was this?

M: During the Depression or a little after. He went for the final interview and he got the job. He was the first Jewish executive at Macy's. He was hired on a temporary basis to see if people could tolerate a Jew. They told him that he had to dress properly. The problem was he had one suit. We were poor. Don't get me wrong, there was always money for rent and food. There was basic security but if you needed to buy anything special, you had to plan it. One suit with two pair of pants took him through college. I guess he wore that suit to the interview and they told him he had to dress better. But he was so bright they couldn't afford not to hire him. My other brother was very different. It was very hard for him to be the younger brother. It was hard to compete with my older brother. My younger brother was more athletic and sociable. He had my mother's disposition and was always surrounded by a million friends. My older brother was always in his room with his books. But they got along well. When my younger brother dropped out of college and went into the military, my father was furious that he'd left school. When he got into officers' training school he said to me, "That'll show Dad that I'm okay." He was a grown man and still felt he hadn't gotten from my dad what he needed. That's an example of how much my dad valued education. He was also a dominant person. Education was important. Again I was lucky because I wanted an education so he thought I was fine and got his approval.

Wasn't it unusual in your day for a woman to get so much education?

M: In high school I had a job at Klein's. I was making a little money and money was important to make, so it was understood that when I got my bachelor's I would work. But I decided I wanted to get a master's in social work. If you can believe it, at Columbia it cost $750 to get a master's and Hunter College was free. I came home my senior year at Hunter College and said that I wanted to get a master's degree. My father said $750 is a lot but if you want to go, we will make it possible for you. He asked both of my brothers to help him with $250 each so I could go. Of course I paid them back. It demeaned my father to ask his sons to chip in, but he did it, because he was so committed to education.

When did you meet your husband, Sol?

I met him after I finished my graduate degree at Columbia. I was the youngest one in the class at Columbia. When I applied, I was 19. In New York if you were good in school, you could skip. I graduated high school at 16 because in addition to skipping, I went to summer school. When I got into Hunter College, I took a test and didn't have to take some beginning level classes and that enabled me to complete my degree quickly.

When did you marry?

M: I married at 22. I was in graduate school at 19. When Columbia interviewed me for grad school, they thought I was too young so I decided I needed to do something to impress them. I got a job in New Jersey working in a home for mongoloid children. That's what children with Down syndrome were called in those days. So I entered Columbia with a little experience in the field I planned to study. I knew I had to do something to get in.

Did you live in New York after you married?

M: No. We got married in July. I wanted to finish my first year of work before we left for our honeymoon, so we left in September. Sol had a car and we were going to Lake Louise in Canada for our honeymoon. I didn't know how to drive and he taught me so I could share the driving. He thought I was real smart and I thought I was real smart. On the way to Lake Louise we got to Montana on Labor Day weekend. I don't know why, but I was driving. I saw this huge Greyhound bus coming toward me and I was petrified. I swerved to the right into an embankment and we had a bad accident. I didn't have a license so Sol said we should change places. I thought I couldn't move, but I crawled over to the passenger side. The ambulance took us to this Catholic hospital in Billings where the staff told us the orthopedic surgeon had just been honored by the pope for outstanding work in orthopedics. Everyone told us how fortunate we were to have this doctor. I was so lucky: I had a fractured pelvis but my doctor had been honored by the pope! The doctor was wonderful and he said, "We will fix you up fine and you'll be able to have children." I didn't even know that was a question. I was stuck in Billings with my feet in a sling attached to the ceiling for six weeks. They'd never had a Jew in this Catholic hospital. It was quite an experience. Once the pain subsided, I felt I was in good hands. I never told my mother. I knew she'd be hysterical so I kept writing letters saying we're having a great time, but we had trouble with the car and couldn't get the right car part. I was receiving the best care and there was nothing they could do so why worry them. Sol wasn't injured so he rented a room and got a temporary job. He joked, "I think I'd make a good Catholic. While you were being operated on, I was in the chapel praying and it worked." That accident and experience pulled us together in a way that was very significant. Sol got a job at a factory. Talk about anti-Semitism. His name, Solomon Smolins, is obviously a Jewish name. The workers had to wear certain clothes to do their job and he arrived one day to find that his co-workers had tied his clothes in knots. But he said, "They're not gonna get to me." That's what he was like. Tough. Unlike the factory, the hospital was great.

What year was this?

M: 1946. That was how we started our marriage.

Did you return to New York after you left the hospital?

M: No. We continued on. We forgot about the honeymoon and took a train down to Denver because Sol's car was demolished. I loved Colorado, which was beautiful. By that time it was October. Sol was an optometrist but Colorado didn't accept his New York license, and they also made it clear that Jews weren't welcome in Colorado as optometrists. They'd had enough of New York Jews. So we left Colorado and came to Texas. In Texas it was different. He went to work for Texas State Optical, which was owned by Jews. We ended up in Beaumont where we had a little rented room. He was working and I was recuperating. But living in a small town didn't suit me. One day I needed a garbage can, so I took the bus to town to buy one. The next day Sol told me that at work someone said something to him about the garbage can. I said, "What?" He said, "This is a small town; everyone knows everything." I said, "Honey, I can't live like that. I'm from New York. Nobody knows anything about anybody." I mean we had neighbors and we'd say hello but nobody went into anyone's apartment. I thought it was terrible that people were talking about my shopping trip. He thought it was funny. I said, "Why don't you see if you can get a transfer?" Anyway, he got a transfer and we ended up in San Antonio. As you see, I didn't steer the boat, but I had a voice in what was going on.

What were your first impressions of San Antonio?

M: I thought San Antonio was really a hick town—no theater, no art. I was a New York snob. But at least there was some possibility of anonymity. When we first settled here, I was a psychiatric social worker at the Red Cross; the veterans returning from the war were in terrible shape. That's back when they used a lot of shock therapy. It was terrible. I had to have keys to get into the locked ward. One day I walked into the ward--you know, cheery, cheery me-- and I asked a soldier if there was something I could do for him. He said he wanted to have sex with me! I said, "Well, I'm not sure I can do that but let me find out."

Well, it's a good thing you were a New Yorker with a good sense of humor and could think on your feet!

M: I worked there for a year then got transferred to a different Red Cross unit. Soon after that, I got pregnant and left and later we had had two daughters. But being a fulltime at-home mother was not enough. It was boring. I mean I loved my kids and I was probably a decent mother, but I wasn't interested in cooking and homemaking projects. In those days that's what the magazines were all about--how to make an eggplant into a flower or how to learn new, fancy domestic skills. It seemed ludicrous and I didn't like it and felt out of tune. When Laurie, my older daughter, was three, I thought she should go to nursery school. That's when we joined the Temple, because they had a good nursery school. But I found the ladies at the Temple were impossible. They were always all dressed up all the time and they were not my kind of women.

Then what happened?

M: I decided I needed to go to work. Wendy was three and Laurie was six. I went to work at the Child Guidance Center. It was a quality place and they liked my degree from Columbia. Here in Texas it was like gold and they accepted the idea that I only wanted to work part time. When I told Sol I really wanted to go to work, he said, "What about the kids?" I said Wendy would be at nursery school and Laurie would be in first grade. He said, "That's fine with me, but I don't want anyone else cooking dinner." I burst out laughing! My cooking isn't much, but he thought it was great. I went to work when the Child Guidance Center was just beginning to operate.

What about Sol's work?

M: First he worked for Texas State Optical on Houston Street. We needed money to buy his own practice so we lived on what I earned and saved his salary so he could buy a practice. At that practice he was the first optometrist in San Antonio to have blacks and whites in the same waiting area. He was the first optometrist to integrate and call black people Mr. and Mrs. Everywhere else optometrists called black patients by their first names. No respect, and I hated the racism. At first I said, "I'll never fit in here." The buses were segregated. The Majestic had an upper floor for the blacks and they couldn't sit down below with everybody else. I couldn't believe it. Every day I got on the bus and sat in the back--you know a big protester--until one day a black lady came up to me and said,"Lady, we really need these seats here. Can you please sit up front?" Poor woman, she'd worked all day and been on her feet and needed a seat and I'm taking her seat. I came home and I said, "There is no place for me in this town. I cannot live here."

And yet you stayed.

M: Well, Sol and I got very involved with trying to make things different. The ACLU was a big part. We had meetings in our house. I remember one meeting at our house that was organized by the ACLU where there were a lot of participants I didn't know. So, I was trying to be a good hostess and make conversation when I asked a black man who was new what kind of work he did. He said, "I hustle." What honesty.

Obviously you and Sol had a real relationship as a couple. Very devoted and on the same page but you've also told me Sol was frequently depressed.

M: That was the hardest part of the marriage. This wonderful guy was depressed long before they knew what to do about it. He hated his medication. It made him drowsy and put him to sleep. He wasn't himself. It was agonizing. There were many terrible periods throughout the marriage; I felt helpless. Here I was with my education and working in a psychiatric setting; I'd ask everybody who knew about depression. I'd talk to people at the med school and I got him in therapy with some psychiatrist who was supposed to be good. I did what I could, but it didn't help. He was smitten with this terrible illness that came unannounced, spent itself, and then he would be better. It came from no apparent cause. He wanted it differently and I wanted it differently and it was sad. I felt helpless. I loved this man and I couldn't help him. There were mornings when he'd say, "I don't think I can get out of bed today." And I'd sit with him and say, "Honey, you did yesterday…"

When did the first episode of depression occur?

M: Not long after we married. The whole marriage was touched by his depression. Talk about his bad luck! I couldn't change it. I couldn't fix it.

If someone asked whether your life has a theme, would it be social justice?

M: That certainly would be a major theme. I like people. I can't imagine a life without people around; they have to be people of my choosing, of course! But I didn't go into social work for no reason. I love what I did, and one of my daughters is a fabulous family therapist.

When were Sol's best periods?

M: Sol was better when we travelled. That was great. We had wonderful times. I've been very lucky to have travelled and visited many places in the world, including China and India. I'm interested in what the people do and how they earn a living, how they live.

How important are friendships with other women?

M: Very. I need people. Men and women. I need people in my life. I'm happiest when there are people in my life. I go to one book group where they don't discuss the book much, but they are nice and it's fun. So I like that. I read on my own; I don't need them for that. I do like people. Life for me is with people.

What's a typical day?

M: It varies. I take classes. I swim, read, see friends.

When you retired, did you have to relearn how to spend your time?

M: Not really. I've always read a lot. I read both fiction and nonfiction. I'm not into mysteries. I want to know about people, and I like to read their stories.

What did you read when you were young?

M: Nancy Drew mysteries. I had a group of girlfriends, and we made a pact that for anyone's birthday we had to give a Nancy Drew book we hadn't read and then we'd pass it around and share it.

Has your recognition of the unevenness of luck given you your desire to even things out a bit?

M: You know my dad's parents were killed in the Holocaust. Life isn't necessarily good. You've got to do something constructive to make sure human rights are respected; when bad things happen, you've got to do something.

Your mother was a great influence on you. Who or what else was?

M: My dad. He wasn't a warm person, but I wanted to please him. He was important. I don't know, how do we know what influences us? Life influences us. There's a part of me that is moderately resilient. I'm resilient. That's nice. I had this accident on my honeymoon and I wrote amusing poetry while I was there and the nuns would laugh. It was fun. I made it fun. The sisters would gather around this Jewish girl's bed and they'd say, "Tell us something." So I'd write funny little poems and they'd laugh. It was a way not to think about all the bad things that could happen. I do love life and my mother loved life. It was disturbing that I couldn't help my husband. It was very humbling. I didn't accept it. It was agonizing and I was going to fix it one way or another but it didn't help. That was difficult. Recognizing you're not all that powerful is humbling. The important thing was that he was a good man and the depression didn't define him. He lived a good life. With problems, no doubt, but he lived a good life. The illness is just a part of the whole, not the whole. Mental health is just the way you are put together; it's not who you are and you've got to get on with life. The way a person is put together does not wholly describe who they are.

Do you see yourself as having made any bad choices in your life?

M: No, I don't think so.

What's the best choice you made?

M: Being alive. Being lucky. Marrying Sol. Having kids. My life has been wonderful. I've been so lucky. The marrow of my bones knows I'm lucky. I read about other people suffering and here I am.

When Iraqi-American Muna AlSalaan first came to the United States for brief periods as a young woman, she liked much about American culture, including women's relative personal freedom. A Muslim who, she says, practices Islam her own way, she finds herself quite unlike many Arab women because of her independent thinking and life. She has helped her children achieve much of what she was unable to because of patriarchal control, and she is currently writing poetry and stories.

MUNA ALSALAAN

First off, I want to say that we are thrilled that you are fluent in English. We thought you might need a translator.

M: I speak English, because I was a teacher and a headmaster years ago. I first came to the United States from Iraq more than 20 years ago. My problem is that I've lost some of my hearing and that affects my speaking skills as well.

Do most of your Iraqi friends speak English?

M: In Iraq we teach children English in elementary school. After I got my degree in Iraq I taught preschool English. When the war started in Iraq in 1991, I decided to leave Iraq and come to the United States, following my daughter who was already here and American. When I came here I started to remember the language so I learned more and more. I was also getting my degree as an assistant teacher.

So, when the war broke out, you left here and returned to Iraq?

M: Yes, I went to see my family and stayed two years during the war with Kuwait. Over the following years, I went back and forth many times and stayed a year or two each time.

I'd like to go back and talk about your childhood.

M: I was born in Baghdad; I have four brothers and three sisters; I was one of the middle children. I was born in a different culture with different traditions.

I assume your mother stayed at home and took care of all of you. What did your father do?

M: He was an elementary school teacher at first. Later he lost his job and still later he became an administrator.

How old were you when you first came to America?

M: I was 25 years old and came with my husband who got a scholarship to study at a university in Chicago. Because I was good in English, I sometimes taught the public. Now my poor husband is in a nursing home. It breaks my heart. He is 86 and has Alzheimer's but otherwise he is healthy.

So, you came here for your husband to study and you stayed?

M: Oh no, we had to return to Baghdad. The Iraqi government had paid for his education so that he would return and work in Iraq. They wanted us to bring our knowledge back.

How many children do you have?

M: Three. Two were born in Iraq and the youngest was born here. When we moved to this country, it opened my mind to the world and I loved America. I wanted to live just like Americans live here, so I was an exception in Iraq. I behaved like an American woman and many Iraqis didn't like that.

Was that true even in the 80s?

M: Oh sure. Even in the 90s. But we went to a special club in Bagdad that was very western. I respect the people in Iraq and I respect Islam-- but in my own way. That's what I wanted for my children.

What did your parents think of that?

M: My father was one of the few educated people in Iraq. Only 5% of the Iraqi population was able to read and write, and my father was a teacher. My mother knew how to read and write but only about religion. She could not read or write a letter. My parents raised all of us to be educated. They were not at all unhappy with my western behavior and dress and love for America. My own son studied in France and moved to Germany where he is now a successful neurologist. One daughter has a master's degree from England. She worked for the United Nations and wrote a book about the effects of war on children. My other daughter attended Bagdad University and now lives here with her family. She got a master's degree in education at Incarnate Word University.

And your husband? What did he do?

M: He was an actor and theater director. I have photos of him with famous Hollywood actors.

When did you move to the United States permanently?

M: In 2003. Before that, I'd gone back and planned to live in Iraq. But when war started again, I left. First I went to Germany to live with my son, but I didn't really like Germany. Germans are different, not like Americans. Besides I know English, not German.

Are Iraqis friendly to foreigners?

M: The people in Iraq are very friendly. Even American soldiers have talked about how friendly the people were to them. In the beginning everyone was happy to get rid of Saddam Hussein. But as the years go by, some people say Iraq was better off under Saddam. Opinions have changed. I think different leaders helped to keep the nation ignorant so the people can't tell the difference between good and bad. It's hard. They don't know what to do.

Was your husband brought up with a western mentality like you?

M: Yes, because if he were not, I wouldn't be like this. Arab men control women. But my husband isn't like that, because his family was educated too. His father was the teacher of my father.

Was your marriage arranged?

M: Yes, it was arranged between our two families. Not by my husband and me. But it worked. It had to. I was a friend of his sister. His family told him they chose me and he knew who I was. I was nineteen and he was twenty-five. He was different than me. He was spoiled; I was ambitious. I was upset because I wanted to study and become a doctor. My mother told my father how sad I was and how I was crying. My mother took me to talk to my father. He said, "Tell me why you don't want to marry." I said, "I want to study, I want to go to college. I want to be a doctor." He said, "I respect his father. I gave him my word." He was telling me how important his teacher was to him. To my father, his teacher was like someone sent from God. My father would not say no to his teacher; he would never say, "I will not give my daughter to your son." I was crying. I knew nothing about this man I was going to marry, and didn't know if the marriage would work. And at that time there was no divorce. I would have to keep silent about any problem that might occur. But I was clever.

Tell us about that, please!

M: I thought my husband would be like my brothers: educated and active and competent. They studied and read and knew how to do things. My husband was not like this. My brothers looked ahead and he didn't. But even though my brothers were educated, they didn't want us women to be free. If I wanted to go out I needed permission. This was the way it was. When it was dark, no girls were out unaccompanied by men. I couldn't stay out after sunset. This was the traditional way. But when I came to my husband to ask him if I could go some place, he said, "You don't need to ask." I liked it. When I wore something and I asked him if it was suitable, he said, "You can do whatever you want." I loved it. When I would report to him where I had been and what I had been doing, he would say, "You don't need to tell me." So I overlooked the parts of him and our life that weren't so good, and focused on the positive parts. My husband was free-thinking and open-minded. He rarely forced his opinion about anything. Sometimes you need and want another opinion. He'd say, "You know. You don't need to ask me." So I started to think for myself and for my family more than ever and worked hard to manage my life the way I wanted it. For this I am very grateful and proud of my husband whom I respect and love.

So you developed yourself.

M: Yes, I read many books.

What did you read?

M: Anything. Everything. My brothers read a lot. When I was little, I would read the books they left out. Even philosophy when I was eleven or twelve. My husband liked to go out a lot. After a while I told him that we were married and needed to spend more time together, so I would go wherever he went. When Saddam came, life started to change. It became more open. The government opened three or four clubs with swimming pools. There were days for women and days for men. We joined a club that was very nice and decided that we'd go sometimes together; other times he would go with his friends. We also had a group of friends we met there. We would dance-- waltz and tango--and drink until morning. This was very different from the rest of the people in Iraq. I told you, maybe 10% of the population. We weren't rich but I was clever. I couldn't afford to buy clothes from the nice shops so I looked at the clothes and then I sewed or knitted. Every Thursday we were at the club from nine o'clock until three o'clock in the morning. There was a band and dancing. It was very classy. Sunday we went for bingo. I needed to dress and do my hair.

So you figured out how to live a high life without a lot of money.

M: Yes, I knew how to live well with less money.

Tell me about the books you read as a child.

M: Egypt was the country that all Arabs looked toward in those years. It was open and educated. It was invaded by Napoleon so they were open to Europe more than us. I was reading their books and magazines. There were some Lebanese writers and we had maybe five famous Iraqi poets. By the way, I am also a writer and a poet. But I couldn't write much because I was busy taking care of the house and children. And I had to decide everything. Sometimes you feel like what you decide may be wrong. I wanted to apply to be a pharmacist or dentist. But my husband wouldn't let me. I had one child who was three and because my husband didn't want to do anything to help me, how could I be at school. I went to my family and I cried to my mother and said my husband wouldn't let me apply. She couldn't do anything. Because when men speak, women have to listen. My mother said, "You have a child. This is your degree." She said that to make me feel better. So I went to school to be a teacher. That was only a one-year course. My husband suggested that I be a lawyer. My interest was in science but he wanted me to be a lawyer. I am more quiet and soft-spoken; to be a lawyer you have to have lungs and be talkative! I told him I didn't I want to be a lawyer and instead studied to be a teacher. I had just one year of study and then I was a teacher all my life. When I was twenty-six years or twenty-seven years old and living in Chicago, I applied to Roosevelt University. Then I got pregnant and once again he said, "I will not help you." An Iraqi actor told my husband that in Iraq they didn't have designers to make clothes for the actors-- let her do this." My husband told him not to mention it. I kept telling him, "Look at me. You didn't let me be a doctor. You didn't let me be a dentist."

So, even when you came to this country he still ruled?

M: Not exactly. He didn't rule but he wasn't involving himself in our affairs. I went to college again before I was forty. I worked really hard to finish college. I studied psychology. I applied to attend university. At that time in Iraq there were only two sections: literature and science. There was no opening in science. A few years later there was an opening and I enrolled, but I couldn't finish. So I worked on my children. I wanted to be a doctor—I couldn't, so I helped my son become a doctor. I wanted to be in college—both my daughters finished college and have master's degrees. All my children fulfilled the hopes I had for myself. I am proud of them and they have good positions in life. My husband was the head of the Art Institute in Baghdad.

How did he do that?

M: He studied and he worked and we were in the right social class. We were invited to embassies and high-class clubs.

Was it his connections that got him the job?

M: No. He received a good degree as a Theater and Actor Director. The Art Institute in Bagdad hired him and he became the head of this Institute. It was the only Art Institute in all of Iraq. He left the work of the house and family to me. He didn't want us to interfere with his time. He left me alone. Sometimes, like I said, we want someone to help make decisions but I didn't have that. I had to do everything. In a way that was good because it gave me more freedom.

So, in a way you were lucky?

M: Yes. My husband is a very good man.

Did you make the decision to move to the United States permanently?

M: Yes. And he didn't come with me. I told him because of the war, Iraq doesn't have food and many other things. Children didn't know anything about bananas, apples or chocolate. You couldn't find any fruit or sweets in the country. This was after the war in Kuwait. 1991. So I told him, "I want to go to America. Why don't we go?" Our son was in Germany, one daughter was here in America, and we had one daughter in Iraq, working in the United Nations. I told him that perhaps she could ask to work in another country. He said, "You go." I thought once I was here he would be alone and couldn't manage. But he didn't come. After a year I had to go back to check on him. People were shocked by my departure. You know, a wife leaving her husband; friends and family blamed me, "How could you leave him alone?" I went back and begged him to please come with me. There were robberies and people were stealing cars. He didn't want to come. I told him I would not come back. There is too much coming and going, too much money spent for travel. After Saddam got killed, my son tried to force my husband to leave Iraq. We asked my daughter to leave because it was dangerous for girls and women; they were being raped. My daughter and her daughters went to Jordan. He still wouldn't go. One day a neighbor called my daughter and told her that her father, my husband, was in the hospital. She went to the hospital and he had almost died. Anyway, she took him to Jordan. I applied for him to come to the United States. It took maybe three years. After the war it was hard to enter this country. When I came here, it was easier. After he came, I saw a change in him I couldn't understand. He was different; I was afraid of him. So I lived with a friend until I could get another apartment. My son saw him and said he was sick.

Was that how you found out he had Alzheimer's?

M: Yes, and then we put him in a nursing home. I didn't want to, but my son insisted.

You are a very strong woman.

M: I've had to be. It was good that my son helped me. I also got to talk about other things with him like science and chemistry.

Do you speak in Arabic together?

M: Yes. I didn't learn German. I knew he would live in Germany, but I didn't learn the language. Saddam wanted to open an Arabic language school in Germany, but Germany wouldn't allow it. So Saddam closed the school in Iraq that taught German.

When did you start writing?

M: When I was thirteen or fourteen years old. Later one of my brothers said, "You are good in mathematics and chemistry. You can be a doctor, so go to science section." When I was fifty I began writing again when I was living in Iraq. I started to write to express my emotions. My husband was behaving differently, and I didn't understand. I started to write about him. I wrote about his behavior.

Did you write stories? Essays?

M: No, poetry. I also wrote some children's books but I couldn't publish any of it because I was busy with my husband. I couldn't find time for myself. And because of difficulties in Iraq when the war with Iran started, everything was very expensive. There were obstacles and Saddam didn't let Iraqis leave because everyone would have left. No Iraqi got out.

So you were trapped?

M: Yes. To work as a writer I needed to meet poets and publishers. Because of the war in Iraq, everything was difficult and expensive. This was hard for me. Since I came to the United States and he came, I couldn't leave him. He needed me to take care of him. I don't write much now. I wrote a poem a few months ago about Baghdad.

Do you write in Arabic?

M: Yes. I have met a few American poets here and read some of my poems to them and they liked them. I read my poem "Marriage Day" and they liked it. A friend translated it for me. It's hard for me to translate Arabic into English. I am afraid I will use wrong words. You have to have more words than I do. I am still planning to write Arabic, English and Spanish poems.

Is there anything you miss about Iraq?

M: Indeed I miss my country and I feel sorry for what has happened. But, as I told you, when I came here: I loved this life. I love the relative absence of family control and the way individuals can think for themselves. I told you the way I got married. The families arranged it. My father decided, not me. I was nineteen; I wanted to study to go to college. I couldn't because of my family. I don't miss much, but I do miss the country itself.

Is there a large enough Arab community here for you to have Arab friends?

M: Yes, but I am different. I think differently. It's hard for me. For people who are traditionally religious, religion is like a circle around you to tell you what to think and keep you from doing wrong. But I don't follow everything in Islam. Even when I was a child I didn't. My mother and father found out when I was a child that I am different. They didn't force me to fast and to pray. Even now I am different. I make my own rules and forms. Muslims have to pray sixteen cycles. I don't do it. I pray my way. Muslim people--Sunni and Shia--I respect them all. I pray some parts like Shia and some parts like Sunni. In the past all Muslims were together, friends. Besides, I go to churches and to synagogues, and I respect all kinds of people. I've joined with people who worship Buddha. I like Buddhist philosophy very much. It's hard for me to find other women from Arab countries who think like me.

My Wedding Day

Original in Arabic, translated into English

I wanted to say a word to you on my wedding day

The day you sprouted my hopes.

And that day, all my sadness vanished.

That day, I was born again

and forgot my sadness.

That day I entered your school and I learned great lessons

and that day you told me:

I am your dreams and your strengths.

I didn't say my word because you were my word and passion,

And I was overwhelmed by you.

https://www.youtube.com/watch?v-TqDHIPnToMo

Diana Carroll-Wirth decided as a young woman to live an untraditional life. As a young woman she had three goals: to write a book, to be in a movie, and to have a French boyfriend. She fulfilled all three dreams. Now retired after a long career with the United States Army and the United States Information Agency (USIA), which enabled her to live and travel abroad, she has decorated her home with folk art from India, Thailand and many other countries. Since retiring in San Antonio, she has served on boards of the Carver and Guadalupe Cultural Centers and continues to use her talent and knowledge to culturally enrich the city.

DIANA CARROLL-WIRTH

What a collection! We don't know where to look first.

DCW: Yes, these are things I collected while I lived around the world. There's a story that goes with nearly everything. I also want to show you a few things before we start. Here are some articles I've written and a list of places I've lived.

Great! Let's get started.

DCW: Since I was very young, there have been certain things I wanted to do in my life. One was to write a book; another was to be in a movie; and a third was to have a French boyfriend. Well, I did all three! This is my book: while I was living in Bombay, I compiled a survey of all the best restaurants there. It's way out of date now, of course, but others have done updates. A colleague and I sampled all those restaurants ourselves; we ate and ate and gained ten pounds each! My Indian colleague went into one of the kitchens, came out, and told me, "You don't want to go into the kitchen. You enjoyed your meal. That's enough." Bombay (Mumbai) is a huge city, the center of India, the stock market center and Bollywood; people from all over India come to Bombay to make their fortune, so our guide was important to many people as the food represented all regions; it served those who wanted the familiar as well as the unfamiliar. Here's an article about my apartment in Bombay. You can see that I've been a collector of folk art, textiles, rugs, and books for many years.

I love the way you hung the rugs on the ceiling.

DCW: It was a nice apartment, but it wasn't big enough for all the stuff I had. Here's an article from Karachi, my last posting. This is from here in San Antonio, written by a woman who used to write the food column. I've lived and traveled many places.

In this article you showed us, I see that your lineage is very mixed. It says your father was Irish, black and Cherokee, and your mother was English, black, and Delaware. What do you consider yourself? Do you have a racial identity?

DCW: I'm a black American. In this country, if you have one drop of black blood you are black. You know that. While I have no reservation experience I have connected with my Delaware tribe in Bartlesville, Oklahoma where I attended a typical outdoor ceremony, which was quite moving.

Do you have enough Indian blood to claim to be a Delaware or a Cherokee?

DCW: I don't know. Everybody in South Carolina is part Cherokee. None of that is who I am. That's who my ancestors were.

Let's start with where you were reared.

DCW: I was born in Chicago, though we lived in Gary, Indiana, where my mother was a teacher and my father, a lawyer. Later they took me back to Gary, Indiana. I was a Depression baby and money was tight. My parents saved their pennies and bought a farm of 85 acres in Michigan. The weekends and summers were in Michigan on the farm, and during the week we lived in Gary, where I went to school. We moved to Michigan permanently when I was in high school. Then I went to Western Michigan College in Kalamazoo and after graduation, worked in Chicago for three or four years as a librarian before I began looking for an overseas job. In those days in order to travel you had to be very wealthy or have a job. So I looked for a job.

When you were a little girl did you dream of the adventurous life that you built for yourself?

DCW: Absolutely! I did not want an ordinary life. There's nothing wrong with that; it just wasn't for me. I was an only child with no extended family; no living grandparents or aunts and sisters and brothers, so an ordinary life wasn't mine, and I didn't want one. My father died when I was 14, and I graduated from college when I was 19.

How did you do that?

DCW:Very simple: I graduated from high school when I was 16 by skipping two grades in elementary school.

Looking back, did your life match the dreams you had as a little girl?

DCW: Don't you make your dreams come true yourself?

Not everybody does.

DCW:You do if you want to. Even people who are physically handicapped or limited by age, class, race or gender can try to grasp what they want.

When I began my academic career, there was still considerable sexism in the academy. When you started in the Foreign Service, did you find sexism was an issue?

DCW: No.

Where were your first postings?

DCW: In 1955 I got a job with Department of Army and began my travels. My first work abroad was as a civilian librarian working for the US Army in France, Germany and Italy. The second part of my career began in 1980 when I joined the United States Information Agency (USIA) and served as a Foreign Service officer in Germany, India, Bangladesh and Pakistan.

Did you have a favorite?

DCW: France. It's the best.

The best food? The best men? The best scenery?

DCW: Thank you. Yes! You answered your own question. As far as Asia, my favorite was India. It was the most colorful place I've ever been in. Crafts, color, food and diversity--good God, India has it. And, interestingly, I learned more about my own country being overseas because I hadn't traveled here much. But as a Foreign Service officer, you are supposed to talk about your country, so I damn well did learn a lot about it. I also did more trips around this country. I did do a little bit of travel in this country by going to graduate school in Berkeley. The Department of the Army had a scholarship enabling civilian employees to get a free year of college education to enhance their job, and you could go wherever you were accepted. I applied to Hawaii, Montreal, UCLA, and Berkeley and the first three accepted me right away. But I didn't hear a thing from Berkeley for months, and the pressure was on for me to pick a school or the scholarship would be taken away. Finally Berkeley came through and that's where I went. I got my BS in librarianship from Western Michigan University in Kalamazoo and my Masters in Librarianship at UC Berkeley.

What credentials were required to apply to be a Foreign Service officer?

DCW: You need to have a college degree. A lot of non-tenured professors love Foreign Service because it allows them to travel and go on to another career path. We had a lot of lawyers, teachers, journalists, and economists. You have to take a daylong written exam as well as another daylong oral assessment and write a personal narrative.

What did your job entail?

DCW: When I was in the Foreign Service I was a cultural affairs officer at USIA. The agency was independent at the time, but now it's a part of the state department. We ran information and cultural centers with libraries around the world. We helped make arrangements for performers from America to perform in the host country as well as college professors to lecture at local universities or meet with their counterparts. A public affairs officer would read the media every day to make sure that what was printed about the United States was correct, and if not, we rebutted it. We interviewed potential Fulbright scholars and chose recipients for U.S universities. That is just a fraction of our duties; our principal duty was to develop mutual understanding between nations.

What aspect of your job did you enjoy the most?

DCW: If you look at this house, you can see that the cultural aspect of travel was the important thing in my life.

The image of a girl from the Midwest going to all these exotic places intrigues me.

DCW: I decided that since I was not wealthy, I had to work overseas. Somewhere along the line I remember someone talking about Foreign Service, but it went in one ear and out the other. I think I didn't pay attention because I thought there was a language requirement. There isn't. You have to be able to *learn* a language but you don't have to already possess language proficiency to apply. One of my colleagues knew several languages, entered knowing Egyptian Arabic and Hebrew and then they kept making her learn other languages so she could be even more versatile. In the Foreign Service, there are hardship posts and non-hardship posts. Europe is not a hardship. India is. Bangladesh is a greater hardship post.

How many languages did you learn?

DCW: German and cooking French. See all my cookbooks? I also learned Italian and it was quite good while I was there. But you know, the Italians are lovely liars and tell you that your pronunciation is good even when it's not. I went from France to Italy and I had just grasped the bottom rung of the French language. I could never gargle out the "r" right. Got to Italy and automatically the brain went into overdrive and I would answer in French instead of Italian. My friends gave me a hard time and reminded me we were not in the part of Italy where they speak a lot of French. But finally I did learn Italian.

Looking at you, I can see that you could pass for a native in almost any country. Did that make it easier for you?

DCW: Yes, I fit in very nicely. In Thailand I was a tall Thai with sunglasses. I met a man there who was happy to dance with me because he had a hard time dancing with the tiny Thai women. I was abroad with my mother who lived to be 97. She was with me the last twenty years of her life, and that gave me a lot of cultural credit because I was going against the cliché about Americans being nasty to our old people, dumping them in nursing homes.

Did your mother die abroad?

DCW: Yes, in Bangladesh. She had an adventurous life and she enjoyed it.

Of all the things you did and had access to…

DCW: Access! Yes, isn't that the best? Working for the army you were not encouraged to go off base. Everything you needed was there, from groceries, movies, bowling alleys, photo labs, elementary schools. So language learning was up to you as well as learning the customs and culture of the host country. But in the Foreign Service you damn well do and you instantly have access to the best of the host country—university presidents, writers, the intelligentsia.

When did you decide you wanted to be in a movie?

DCW: When I was a little girl. And I did it. Have you heard of Merchant Ivory films? Ishmael Merchant is an Indian, and when I lived in India, we became friends. I invited him to dinner one night and cooked a recipe from his cookbook.

That was brave.

DCW: Yes it was. And he commented that what I made tasted different and I told him I'd added cinnamon, and he said, "You really have nerve, girl" I loved it. We became good friends and I told him I wanted to be in a movie, so he arranged for me to be an extra in a movie he was working on, called "A Perfect Murder." It was a terrible movie, but one of the technical staff told me I was the best extra and I hit my marks! I even got to go to the premiere and walk the red carpet in a sari.

Do you still have goals, things you want to do?

DCW: For one thing, I am working on my memoirs.

Did you take a lot of photos during your years abroad?

DCW: Yes, but I don't really know how to convert them from slides and snapshots. I've got wonderful photos of all kinds of places. The pictures are here but I still need to write the book.

When you retired in 1994, what made you choose San Antonio?

DCW: I was looking for no snow, nice people, airport, foreign films, and a good library. God knows, I love our red enchilada library

During your time in all these foreign places did you ever come up against anti-American attitudes?

DCW: No, but look, most of the issues that create anti -American attitudes weren't happening when I was in the service. I don't know if we were loved then, but we were tolerated and respected up to a point.

Did you ever find yourself in a dangerous situation?

DCW: No. You just have to use commonsense. There were some countries where I had to go into areas that weren't so nice, but I used my head. For instance, many of the places I liked to shop were right next to the red light districts.

Did you ever get ill?

DCW: Yes, the worst was at a formal diplomatic dinner in Bombay. It put me in a hospital. This was the best hospital in Bombay. I had a roommate in my hospital room who had a woman sleeping on the floor beside her bed. It was the daughter-in-law, and this was expected. That's the culture. I talked to a lot of western women who had married Indian men and lived in India. Unfortunately they had some bad Indian mothers-in-law. There's no privacy in India in a normal communal family. You do not shut the door. You keep the door open or everyone thinks something is wrong with you. There was one exception that we knew of. A woman my mother knew married an Indian man who hated his mother and didn't expect his wife to be subservient to her. It was very unIndian behavior. His mother must have been an awful woman.

You experienced many cultures and cultural differences. Was there one you admired or one you thought was the worst?

DCW: There were thousands of worsts. The masculine-dominated societies are terrible for women. You wonder how the women put up with being treated like beasts of burden.

Were you eager to return to the US?

DCW: Yes. When you are in the Foreign Service when you turn 65, that's it. You are out. You might be the best in the city or area where you are, but there are thousands of other people around the world who are also very talented and have the same credentials and are younger. So they are eager to take your place.

What did you do to keep your job and be competitive?

DCW: I wrote well and fast and took care of my boss. I quickly adapted culturally, trained my staff to take my job and was appreciative of their efforts. I learned how to justify things that I wanted. That's kind of a life lesson. Justify the things that you want: a job, a boyfriend, a career. Even a sports car! With the top down! I'll tell you how I got it. Those were the days when you paid two thousand dollars for a car. A friend had to sell his car because his pregnant wife could not fit in the XKE; she gave him an ultimatum—the car or her. So he gave me a very good deal. He had to go buy a family car and I got the convertible. I went to Paris every weekend. It was about a two-hour drive and the car knew the way.

It sounds like you've been all over the world.

DCW: No, I lived only in Asia and Europe with side trips to Africa.

Was there a place you wanted to go that you didn't go?

DCW: No. Oh yes, I forgot! I do have a bucket list: Angkor Wat. You couldn't go when I was in Thailand next door to Cambodia as there was bombing. So that's where I haven't been that I really want to visit.

Looking at your enormous collection of cultural items from all over Asia, I'm wondering, can you still remember where and when you bought it each thing?

DCW: Yes. They are part of my memories.

When you moved to San Antonio how did you meet people?

DCW: I joined organizations I cared about and served on several boards. I was a volunteer at SAMA and part of a group that went to Mexico to shop for things to sell at Bazaar Sabado. I was a Board member of the Guadalupe Center and the Carver Center. That was fun. I was on the committee that hired the entertainment for the year, so I went to New York and spent days watching and listening to various performers and helping to decide which acts were appropriate for the Carver. We paid our own airfare but some of our expenses were paid for by the Doris Duke foundation. I also went to Argentina, Brazil and Canada while I was on the Carver board. I learned a lot about how difficult it is to schedule the wonderful entertainment that comes to this town.

What do you do now?

CW: I belong to the Foreign Service Group, the San Antonio Council of International Visitors, and the University Round Table. I think the chancellor at Trinity started it years ago. You have lunch and there's a speaker or the group goes on a field trip to visit something pertinent. One time they went to the Toyota factory. When I helped schedule events, I scheduled all the people I wanted to meet.

What excites you and energizes you these days?

DCW: I was in the hospital for several months last fall and winter, so just getting out of bed excites me. I'm very happy simply going to a movie or an exercise class.

Are you currently married?

DCW: Yes, for thirty years to a man I met in Stuttgart. He's German and has dual citizenship.

What did your mother think of your life?

DCW: I graduated from high school and went to college when I was 16, so she was used to me being gone. And later, I made sure she was with me. She was a very smart woman and taught for years. We were living in Berkeley when I got the orders to go to Thailand and she was very happy to live in Asia. I always made sure I knew where she could go to church wherever we were. Sometimes it was just a chaplain on a military base.

What do you read?

DCW: Look at all my travel books, and over there are cookbooks, and another collection of art books. I like to read about arts and crafts and the people who make them.

Do you ever lend items from your collection to museums?

DCW: No, I don't know if anyone knows I have it. I would love to. What do you suggest? I do have a collection of autographs that might be interesting for other people to see. For a National Library Week years ago I organized something called Readers are Leaders and wrote to celebrities and asked them to tell me the importance of reading in their lives. I got the most wonderful answers from all over the world including from Ben Gurion who put his letter in a paper bag with a stamp. How's that? Princess Grace responded as well as actors and writers. My staff was very surprised and thought it was a joke! I've shown some of them here at a local branch library. Some of the costumes I've collected could be exhibited at the Central Library. I don't know. I've not really thought about it.

I'm sitting here at this magnificent table in this warm room and imagining a great meal. Do you enjoy entertaining?

DCW: Oh, yes. I'm on the San Antonio Council for International Visitors. The US State Department picks people to come to the US for 30 days, so every embassy has a list of people we believe should see our country; it's a PR thing. It's not a first class trip. It's a way for people to see what America is like and the visits are tailored to the interests of the person traveling. The home hospitality, the connection with Americans in their homes, is what really stays with people. I have written handbooks for Asian travelers explaining some of our cultural differences like our attitudes toward animals: they are part of our families, not food. That Americans tend to be more punctual. Eight o'clock is eight o'clock not ten or ten thirty. We had a group of Japanese visitors recently and had a reception at Incarnate Word. It's a very nice organization. When foreigners come, we set up their professional visits and arrange the home hospitality. The whole point is to break bread with one another and see how we live.

When you have them in your home, do you have a signature dish?

DCW: It depends on the visitors and their culture and desires. So, it's always different. Hindus won't eat beef, Muslims won't eat pork. A favorite unifying dish is macaroni and cheese with lots of chili peppers, but I had a vegan one time who asked if there were eggs in the pasta. I really enjoy it.

You have had such an exciting life.

DCW: I told you I didn't want an ordinary life. And I have no regrets.

Some of the stories you've told us about your life in the Foreign Service suggest that you had quite a bit of clout and power. Was it difficult to resume civilian life?

DCW: Not really. No clout and no power. I had enough sense to know that real life doesn't include staff and help as I was accustomed to. None of that went to my head. It wasn't my life; it was a part of my life. All of the perks I had were so I could do my job well without worrying about the mechanics of living. I knew I wasn't entitled to a driver, a cook, and a person who cleaned the kitchen. That's one of the things I was talking about before. Some people from India, for instance, are lost without all their servants. It takes them a while to get the tea themselves as Americans do.

At 85, is life pretty much what you thought it would be at this time in your life?

DCW: Yes, because I lived with an elderly mother. I got to see what it's like to get older.

Do you have any wisdom you want to impart?

DCW: No! Well, yes: do what you enjoy and if you can't, try to make whatever it is you are doing enjoyable. Figure it out. Liven it up. Make it interesting. I believe in having dreams and figuring out how to fulfill them.

After receiving a BFA and MFA when she was middle aged, Marilyn Lanfear developed into a nationally recognized artist working with an amazing variety of materials. She calls herself a "visual storyteller" and tells her stories using paint, lead, wood, buttons, handmade paper and quilts; she learns whatever techniques she needs for each project. Her current project is an installation about her grandmother which, given her astonishing previous work, might include a lead dress, wood shoes, and a chair made out of handmade paper. Her home, which contains some of her own work as well as her many collections of various objects, is as fascinating as a museum

MARILYN LANFEAR

Wow, let's start with looking at your pieces. You said you've started donating some of them to different institutions. Who's interested in this paper dress?

ML: It's one of my favorites, and the Southwest School of Art is interested. The McNay has taken others. This is a paper copy of my mother's chair.

How did you learn how to construct a chair out of handmade paper?

ML: I took a class in papermaking, which taught me how to make a nice piece of flat paper. I thought, "Well, that's nice but anybody can do that." So then I started making these shapes. Follow me and I'll show you the real chair. This was Mother's chair. The one I made isn't exactly like this, but it's how I remembered it.

So the paper chair is made from a childhood memory. Look at this room. Your house itself is like a museum not just of your own work but also of the things you collect.

ML: I recently had to take everything out of the attic and I've been going through many, many pieces. These are children's huipiles. This one was attached to a saint. Some are for children and some are for saints. Traditionally, a young girl would give the first little dress she made to the saint at her church.

Did you collect them when you traveled?

ML: Yes.

What is that curtain made of? Wood? Wood?!

ML: There were two on either side of the window and they were part of a piece of wood that I carved. It was my first carving project.

It looks so soft…like wool. How did you learn to carve?

ML: I just did it. I learned how to carve wood and solder lead because the story required it. I'm always having to learn a new skill. I learned to carve in order to make cabinets that resemble curtains like this one. I painted each cabinet with old-fashioned milk paint, and each cabinet contained articles to honor a family member's unique quality or interest. For example, my grandmothers' cabinet held 92 thimbles for her age and domestic expertise.

So mostly you've taught yourself how to do everything?

ML: Yes, I've learned from someone and then done it. That took me a long time. When I got my degree from UTSA, I was a printmaker. The collection of drawings you see up there is what I did during that time.

So you started as a print maker and then you became everything else! Is there a medium that you haven't worked in?

ML: I've never worked with clay and I don't know why. I have a feel for it. Just never have. This piece is a copy of a photograph of a gown I wore when I was a child. There's a picture of my brother and me in these gowns that my mother made. I made another one that was the boy's outfit, and it is hanging at the Blood and Tissue Center.

That's paper? It looks like felt. Amazing. Is that the button piece that was at San Antonio Museum of Art?

ML: No, this is the first one I did, but over here is the one you remember. This is my grandmother and there's her husband in the portrait and these are my father and my Aunt Opal and Aunt Ella Mae. My grandmother married again and she had another child and she's represented there. The buttons are all mother-of-pearl except for those brown ones in the afghan. They are made of cattle bones. I met a man once who said when he was a boy there were big piles of bones, piles taller than a one -story building waiting for the train to pick them up. Some enterprising people collected the cattle bones and sold them to button makers.

So everything here represents something from your family and childhood memories. You have so many collections. Are those antique ironing boards?

ML: Yes.

And I saw chairs hanging in the porch room and I see all the miniature chairs here.

ML: I have a lot of collections. I had a beautiful collection of tools that I recently gave to the University of Texas for the architects' building. Over here is a chair I built for a performance piece. Two people who are related wear it. They each have to put an arm around the other and then they perform. I wrote the script and did it here at the craft center and have done it twice in New York. I've done several pieces with this device. It's called "The Chairperson."

Are you working now?

I'm doing several things but I work very slowly. I did a series of wooden pieces when I learned to carve. This is the first piece I made that actually functions. It's a cabinet and I use it for glasses. Originally it held little bottles in which I put sand from beaches all over the world. My friends helped me collect the sand when they traveled. I had all different colors of sand, some from very remote places.

How did that idea ever occur to you?

ML: I don't know. But I needed to do that.

Is the food so beautifully arranged on your kitchen table food that you eat or is it simply beautiful?

ML: It's food I eat. And here are rocks from a place where I used to live near Boerne. I pick up rocks all the time and then I found these fossils. Every time it rained, I'd walk along the highway and pick them up. That's from a series of hats women in my family wore. I think I made one to copy hats worn by probably 20 women in my family. Do you want to go back to my studio?

Of course. Your yard is lovely. How long have you lived here?

ML: Twelve years. I meant to only stay a month but I couldn't find anything that fit me better. That's part of the piece that goes with the wooden curtain you saw in the house. And there are more carved cabinets. I've given a couple to my children.

How many children do you have?

ML: Two sons and two daughters.

Are any of them artists as well?

ML: Yes, one daughter is a dancer and the other designs and manufactures children's clothes. She recently changed to designing and decorating houses. That paper piece hanging there is a copy of pajamas my brother wore. This is a collection of "what not" shelves. It's not in order. When the men who work for me brought it back from where it was exhibited, they hung it out of order. This is just a part of my collection. I have more than 100. Some are from Mexico.

Do you go through phases of collecting? Or do you collect a multitude of things simultaneously?

ML: Some collections start and end, and others go on. This one continues. I have my eye on another shelf.

Tell us a little about your childhood.

ML: I was born in Waco and lived there during my early years. On December 7, 1941 when I was in the fourth grade, we heard on the radio about the attack on Pearl Harbor, the family got in the car, and moved to Corpus Christi. During my adult years I've lived in Eugene and Portland for about 5 years, while I taught at Lewis and Clark and the University of Oregon. And I lived in New York City for about 5 years. I thought I needed to go to Mecca. I loved living there but it was very expensive and I had to live frugally. Most of the time I worked in a gallery during the day and made art in a studio in SoHo in the evenings. It was exhausting but wonderful. I exhibited a little and did performance art.

Look at this table! It's paper! So much of your art looks like something other than what it is materially. They look softer or harder than what they are.

ML: This is an installation piece I'm putting together now.

Installation art is so popular now. Did you grow into it or were you a pioneer?

ML: I guess I was a pioneer.

So you say you moved into this house planning to stay for a month and then stayed 12 years. What happened?

ML: I was going to buy something but couldn't find anything I liked as much, so I still rent this.

When did you start earning a living as an artist?

ML: Before I went back to school, I was selling things but not earning a living. I went to UTSA shortly after it opened and got a BFA and an MFA in the '70s. Then I got a job teaching at SAC and at the Art Institute.

How old were you when you went back to school?

ML: I can't remember exactly, middle aged--my children were grown.

Were you making art when you children were at home?

ML: Yes. But not as much as when I was devoted to it. We had built a big house and my husband suggested we turn the laundry room into a studio but I didn't. I rented a studio downtown.

So, you were born in Waco and later lived in Corpus Christi. Has your family been in Texas for generations?

ML: Yes, that chair over there is from a family member who came to Texas in a covered wagon in the 1800s.

Where did you go to college?

ML: When I was "college age" I went to UT in Austin, but I got married before I graduated. My husband did graduate though with a law degree.

When do you think you hit your stride as an artist?

ML: I think when I made that big button piece. Or maybe when I made the quilt for the Artist and the Quilt exhibit at the McNay. The artists designed the quilts and quilters made them. I met a lot of well-known artists during that show.

Where have you shown?

ML: That particular show was exhibited around the country in about 15 museums.

As I look around, I see so many different art forms—women's hats carved from limestone, a dress made from lead. Did you learn how to weld to construct that sculpture?

ML: Not welding but soldering. I did several pieces like that.

Is most of your work in private collections or museums?

ML: Mostly private, but I am in a few museums. San Antonio doesn't have many collectors and the ones here mostly like to buy in New York or other places that have reputations as important art places. Similarly, I found out when I lived in New York that we here in San Antonio have a lot of interesting theater that doesn't get much recognition.

When you make your pieces that tell family stories do you refer to a diary or notebook or just memories?

ML: I use my memories and make some of it up. I've written stories about some of the pieces. I was going to do a book with a photo of each piece and the story that goes with it. I tell stories, family stories. They are deliberately specific but intended to be universal. When you call a narrative trilogy, "Uncle Clarence's Three Wives" you are being about as specific as you can be.

On your website (marilynlanfear.com) you describe yourself as a "visual storyteller." Do you come from a family of storytellers?

ML: Yes, my father was a storyteller. He told stories about previous generations. That's where the story of the chairperson came from. He used to tell us a story about himself and a friend; one time they caught a bunch of snakes, put them in a burlap sack, and tried to sell them to a carnival. But the carnival owner wasn't interested so they put the bag of snakes back in the car. While they were driving into the country to release them, the snakes got loose in the car. His friend got out of the car while it was moving--he just stepped out of the car! You know those cars didn't go very fast in those days. But it took Daddy longer to realize what was happening; he said it took him what seemed like hours to put on the brake and get out of the car.

Do you have a favorite medium?

ML: No. Whatever I'm working on is my favorite.

Do you begin the work from a story or the medium?

ML: They come together somehow. I started working in lead because my brother who is an architect brought me this lump of lead and said I'd probably be able to figure out something to do with it. So, I made a dress. Often, when I have something to say, I ask myself, "What is the best way to say it? Should I use handmade paper, mother-of-pearl buttons, wood, or lead?"

Who else would think to make a pretty dress out of a lump of lead?!

ML: I had to learn how to hold the lead and the soldering tool and work. Generally, I worked with it down low. When I draw, I work on the floor…not so much anymore because I can't get up. When I had cats, it was a problem because the cats would walk across my drawings.

You are so adventurous and fearless in your choice of subjects and methods. Have you surprised yourself?

ML: No, I just do it. If I need to do it, I do it. In fact that's what I said one time: that I just get someone to show me how to do what I don't know.

Have you ever come across something that seemed impossible?

ML: No. I just do it. I get someone to tell or show me how and then I do it. That doesn't go over well in the academic world. Academics aren't so adventurous. They often didn't appreciate my openly saying that I didn't know how to do some things they could do, like building a kiln. But I was willing to learn.

Is there a project you want to do now?

ML: Yes, I'm working on something about my grandmother. I've got the sewing machine in the studio and a dress and I've collected a number of tools I can use. I haven't figured out the shoes. I just now remembered something interesting: I was going to a dance in high school or junior college and we were to dress as a song. Do you remember the song, "I'm Going To Dance With The Dolly With The Hole In Her Stockings"? Well, Mother made me an old fashioned dress and I borrowed shoes from a woman who worked at the store, oxfords. Mother thought of that. I always thought my father was the artist because he could draw. He taught me to draw a face when I was tiny. I always knew that I wanted to be an artist because I could draw. I thought I inherited my artistic view from him but it was really Mother who knew how to do all these things. My mother could make things, fix all kinds of things, and perhaps most important: she could figure things out. She always had bars of soap for my kids to carve when they came to see her. We collected pinecones and made flowers. She could do anything she thought of but it wasn't "art." And she was an expert seamstress. I didn't inherit that. I could make a dress by a pattern but I didn't really learn how to sew until I was using that lead when I had to manipulate and design it into a dress. Mother could do all that. We used to go downtown together and look in all the windows before I was going to a big party; I would draw the dress I liked and my mother would make it.

Have you designed clothes since then?

ML: No, but that's what my daughter does. And once she learned to sew, she made all of her own clothes from then on.

Has there been anything you needed to overcome?

ML: No, other than the fact I'm a woman and there are more opportunities for males. It has improved but it's been hard. And I think on the whole, men's art is taken more seriously. Maybe not so much anymore.

Have you mentored other women artists?

ML: Yes, in fact a woman was just here helping me with something. She was an art student but now earns her living as a nutritionist or dietician… anyway, she made me a cake for my birthday.

You just had a birthday? How old were you?

ML: I can't remember. I lost track. I thought I'd always know because I was born in 1930 but I still can't remember. Well, I guess I just don't care. Except for the fact that since I had a heart attack I don't have the strength I used to and I have to go to the doctor all the time. I just noticed that change last year.

You've had a healthy life?

ML: Yes, and I've been fortunate. I've lived as if I have money even when I haven't. I am a painter, sculptor, woodworker, performance artist, and collector—and I've left out some things, I think.

That's an artistic life. And look at the beauty you surround yourself with.

Beginning her education in a two-room segregated school, Marie Thurston completed her Ph.D. after she was 70, then was hired by the college president to write the history of St. Philip's College, and now serves as an active trustee of the Second Baptist Church. In their spacious apartment overlooking the San Antonio Riverwalk, she and husband have prints and paintings by important African American artists, a Steinway grand piano, and a wonderful view.

MARIE THURSTON

Let's start from the beginning of your life.

MT: I was born in 1931 in Lynchburg, Virginia, the middle child of three other girls and three boys. At that time, people had large families, all of whom were born at home, delivered by a midwife. My family home was down the road from Jerry Falwell, although I did not personally know his family. During that time in our history, blacks and whites did not fraternize.

Please tell us more about your family and childhood.

MT: I consider myself very blessed, for although my parents had little in the way of formal education, they were very wise. I believe that my father and mother only completed grades three and five. I'm not sure which one went to fifth grade, probably my mother. When I attended elementary school, our schools consisted of elementary grades 1-7 and high school grades 8-11; no kindergarten and no grade twelve. We attended a two-room school with no inside plumbing, no running water, no central heat or air conditioning. My own family did not have running water in our home until after I graduated high school. That was the case in many homes in the 1930s and 1940s in Virginia, both black and white.

Please tell us about your parents.

MT: My mother was a housewife all her life; with seven children and few modern appliances, she had her hands full. I remember that when I was very young, an iceman delivered blocks of ice to keep food cold in an icebox.

And your father?

MT: Although my father had limited formal education, he was quite smart and read all the time. In fact, he subscribed to the Lynchburg newspaper, and we always had several magazines delivered to our home. I remember a weekly newspaper called "The Afro-American" that he subscribed to as well. He worked in a paper mill on three rotating shifts. When he retired from the paper mill, he took a correspondence course in radio and television repair. This was in the late 1940s. He built a small one- story building that was still standing the last time I went back to Virginia. Dad opened his own shop repairing radios and televisions for both blacks and whites in the neighborhood and in the city when he could get the business. He also built the log house I grew up in; it is still inhabited and still beautiful, though it is more than 80 years old. Dad built it to last and it has! My Dad told me that he had promised my mother he would build her a brick house but then he saw a photo of a log house and he loved it, so he and my maternal grandfather went to Long Mountain, and together they cut and skinned the logs and brought them back to Lynchburg. With the help of one of the carpenters in our neighborhood, they built the home I grew up in.

Did your parents stress education?

ME: Oh yes. Every night during dinner my parents asked all of us what we had learned in school that day. My sisters, brothers and I were expected to finish high school and go to college even though there was no money for such an undertaking. My father always told me I could do whatever I wanted to do. Having a father tell you something like that is particularly inspiring. It gives you a kind of confidence that sustains you throughout your life. By the time I had graduated from high school, my two older sisters attended college. One became a registered nurse and the other earned a master's degree in social work. My sister who is younger than I earned a master's degree in education. She retired from teaching in New York City. I can't recall being encouraged by anyone in my school to attend college.

In addition to education, was going to church emphasized?

MT: We were expected, no **required,** to attend both Sunday school and church and if we did not go to church, there was little hope of going anywhere else. Dad was a deacon and the Sunday school superintendent and also served as a trustee in the church. This was a small community where both blacks and whites lived but did not socialize together. We did not go to play with other children except perhaps on Sunday after church. With seven children at home, we always had a playmate and times were different. We all had chores to do as soon as we were old enough, and we all found jobs of some kind or other. When I finished high school, I worked in a black-owned dry cleaning establishment. I worked there for two years before I could save enough to attend Virginia Seminary, a school in Lynchburg (still in existence) that trains black ministers. The school had a two-year school of education, called a junior college, and that is what I attended. I transferred to Virginia State, the state college for blacks, after two years. It cost $375 a year for tuition, room and board, and it was very hard to put together that amount. Financially, Dad could only help a little, but his encouragement meant the world to me. My mother and father were very proud when I finished college. I wish they had lived long enough to see me receive a Ph.D. from the University of the Incarnate Word.

Where did you meet your husband?

MT: I met Charles at Virginia State College, now Virginia State University. He was a year ahead of me but a couple of years younger than I; Charles skipped a grade or two in the early grades, came to Virginia State at 15 and graduated at nineteen. After we married, I had four daughters before I was thirty, so my twenties were busy with raising a family.

Did you support him through medical school?

MT: I helped because I always worked and we lived frugally. Because Virginia was a segregated state, when Charles applied to the University of Virginia Medical School, he was not accepted, so he went to graduate school at Howard University for a year and then reapplied to the University of Virginia. The University was still not accepting black students but they offered him tuition assistance to go to Meharry, a black medical school in Nashville, Tennessee where he graduated as the top student with an all A average. While a junior at Meharry, Charles joined a program offered by the military, and interned in the Air Force in El Paso and then had a four-year military tour in England. After that, he attended the University of Michigan department of dermatology and was selected as their first black Chief Resident. Then we began our first overseas military assignment which included four years in England, four years at Andrews AFB in Maryland near Washington D.C. and four years in Germany. We both enjoyed the military life and the people we met. After living in Germany for years, Charles was assigned to Lackland AFB in San Antonio for his last assignment. Those years in the military gave us many, many opportunities to travel and to befriend people in different countries.

Please tell us about your own graduate school career.

MT: In 1979, I earned a second master's degree from UTSA; years later I was delighted when my daughter told me that Incarnate Word College was starting a Ph.D. Program and she invited me to apply along with her. I did, and at the age of 71, I earned a Ph.D. in Education. One of my daughters and I were in the first cohort! My dissertation was a nation-wide study of African-American women who earned their doctorate after the age of fifty. One of the people I contacted was Dr. Angie Runnels, then President of St. Philip's College. It so happened that she received her Ph.D. before she was fifty, but meeting her proved to be a fortuitous connection. Later, she offered me a job teaching students at St. Philip's who were attending college for the first time. But before I started, she called and offered me something else. She wanted me to write the history of St. Philip's College. I thought about the offer for about ten seconds and said, "Sure I would love to." The main reference source I had was a dissertation written by Clarence Norris Jr., a son of the former dean. Dr. Runnels assembled an advisory committee from St. Philip's who suggested that I gather as much information as I could by interviewing people with a connection to St. Philip's. I began interviewing former students, faculty, administrators and anyone else I could find with a connection to the school. I was amazed at how willing people were to talk about their experience. When I agreed to write the history, I had no idea how many hours of work were involved. But if I were ever tempted to give up, I could hear my father's voice, telling me I could do it and I'd continued working. I know my parents would be proud of my book and be happy to know that I have a master's in guidance and counseling, a second master's in child development, and a doctorate in education. I always studied when we lived overseas and took classes everywhere I lived because I absolutely lo-o-o-o-o—ve going to school.

How did you get into child development?

MT: I was working for the Department of Human Resources. I had a master's in counseling but not in child development. I thought if I'm going to work and progress in this department I should have a degree in it, so I studied for one. We trained people working in daycare centers, inspected the centers, put on workshops and showed the childcare workers how to teach the children. I was with the department for five years. Then our department budget was cut; child development was considered a frill! I saw an ad in the newspaper for a counselor and when I called, the woman I spoke with practically hired me over the phone. But when I showed up for the interview she took one look at me and said they had already filled the position.

That must have been hurtful and infuriating. But I gather you were not about to give up.

MT: I really wanted to work and kept looking for possibilities. I read an article about running a resale shop and thought, "I can do that!" The woman in the article was selling franchises but I thought why pay somebody for something I can figure out myself. While I worked for the Child Development Center, I had heard about a resource where successful retired business people would help beginners like me to establish and run a business. I was introduced to a very special and successful man who had owned a high-end women's shop in Alamo Heights. He could not have been more helpful to me, and he was my friend until the day he died. The night before I opened my first shop, he came by and told me the labels weren't correct, so I stayed up all night and re-labeled every article in the store! He knew I was serious and worked hard, and he introduced me to many people and made many useful suggestions. I opened one shop in 1979 and ran it for five years; I sold it and opened another shop and ran it for eight and a half years.

How did you feel about working in retail?

MT: It doesn't matter what you do, and in fact I loved it! I ran a good business and was honest with my customers. We never told people they looked good in something that didn't suit them just to make a sale. After I closed the second store, I worked as the office manager in my husband's practice and then went back to university to earn my Ph.D.

You've never been a lady of leisure, have you?

MT: I never wanted to be. We have to keep moving!

I am sure you and Charles emphasized education with your four daughters.

MT: Of course. It was never a question of whether they would go to college, just where. And that is also true of our ten amazing grandchildren, who have numerous degrees! I remember a time when I prayed that God would allow me to live long enough to see our daughters finish high school—not college, high school. My God was indeed too small at that time. Not now. Now I am just deeply thankful.

When did Charles retire from the military?

MT: When he was 42, Charles retired on a Friday and then opened his medical practice the following Monday! He had two very long careers and just retired from private practice in 2014. When we first settled in San Antonio we lived in the suburbs, in Windcrest and joined the neighborhood church where there were only three black families who were members. We loved the people, the Sunday school, and the services and certainly grew spiritually there. But when we moved to this apartment in the center of the city, we were intentional about joining a black church.

How have things changed in race relations during your lifetime?

MT: When I grew up we rode on the back of the bus. Finding employment for females that did not involve domestic work was rare, and it was no easier for African American males. They were offered only the menial jobs. I can recall leaning on a fence looking at a swimming pool in Lynchburg where I grew up and thinking how nice it must be to be able to swim. Where I lived we didn't have swimming pools for blacks or access to a lot of other amenities. There were black schools and white schools; everything was segregated, including churches.

What do you think about life in your 80s?

MT: It's wonderful. I haven't been bored yet. Only this year I have slowed down. Age was always just a number to me until this year when I had back surgery. Suddenly I realized that I couldn't do all the things I used to do. For the first time in my life, I had to use a wheelchair in the airport on our vacation this year. But I am much better now and able to walk long distances and work all day. I work out at a gym and have a trainer. That Charles and I live in this wonderful condo is a God thing. I know I am here because this is where God put me. We saw a presentation about this building when it was being built, and I was intrigued by the idea of living on the Riverwalk. We called the developer a couple of days later and purchased what is still our home. We were young then, in our forties. It was 1979. When we moved here, we used to run on the Riverwalk; now we walk slowly. When we sold our house in Windcrest, the children complained that we were selling their home. Now when we talk about selling this condo, they say the same thing.

Are you a profoundly religious person?

MT: Very much. I'm quite certain God has had and still has a hand in my life. When we moved to this condo we couldn't decide where to go to church. We are surrounded by many churches in this neighborhood, but in the end we chose a church on the east side because we thought we could be of more service to a black church. The Second Baptist Church is a wonderful church with a wonderful minister. The church has recently built a community center with a gym, a bowling alley, classrooms, a computer room, and a stage. It's an old church with many senior citizens, but the center is to serve the whole community. We have an excellent after-school program. I serve on the trustee board of the church and we are in charge of maintaining the building and the grounds.

Your father was a trustee in his church and you are a trustee in yours! And what could demonstrate your belief in God more than giving back the way you do?

Known as "the mother of Yoga in San Antonio," Esther Vexler brought yoga to generations of people in the city as well as being one of the most dedicated volunteers and philanthropists. As part of her volunteer work, she invited troubled teenagers into her home years ago; these days when she sees them they are often successful members of the community—and full of gratitude for her. Now 98, she talks about "giving back" rather than giving, continues to inspire yoga students using only her voice, and answers every "how are you?" with one word: grateful.

ESTHER VEXLER

We're so very happy to have an interview with you for our book of interviews with lively, interesting women over 80 years old.

E: Eighty seems so young. I think that at 80, I was teaching 12 yoga classes a week. Eighty seems young when you're 97 like me!

Not everybody knows how wonderful women are at 80+.

E: That's true. Age isn't the end.

Weren't you called Baby when you were quite young, since you were the youngest of nine siblings?

E: Yes, and later I was called Bitsy and finally I'm Esther.

What memories from your childhood are in your head today?

E: One of the thoughts that keep coming back to me is that we had a German shepherd, called Queenie, who was like a family member. She'd jump up and put her paws on my shoulders, but she was so gentle she wouldn't knock me down. In those days there were no dog trainers but she knew how to sit and follow and she saved our lives several times. For example, my mother left her iron on one day and Queenie smelled smoke and got us out of the house.

What else do you remember from your early years?

E: In my youth the Jewish community in and around San Antonio was small. Jews from places like Seguin would come to San Antonio for business or to go to Temple Beth El and they would often stay over at our house rather than drive home in the dark. Our house, like many houses in those days before air-conditioning, had a sleeping porch. I never knew where I was going to wake up in the morning. I'd go to sleep in my bed and often be carried asleep into another room to make room for someone else who was spending the night. We had about five beds on the sleeping porch. It was pretty much ongoing because people would come into town for business and appointments as well as events. People came from as far as Abilene. It was such a different time. We never locked our doors or carried keys. San Antonio was a small town.

So you were born right here in San Antonio?

E: I was born in Santa Rosa hospital. Harold, who recently died--my husband of almost 74 years-- was born in Montreal. His father came from Europe on a ship and planned to come to America but the ship dropped him in Montreal. My parents were both born in Germany but they came when they were young. My mother was 5 and my father was probably 9. They met and married in St. Louis. It was about the turn of the 20th century. When I was born, the family lived on Fir St. It was just a narrow street and then they moved to 327 Army Blvd. The house is still there. I went to Ben Milam #4 grammar school. It's now the headquarters for San Antonio Independent School District. (SAISD) It was just across the street from Fort Sam Houston Army Post. I used to get a ride to school on the post wagon, which was led by horses. The postmen let me off at the corner of my school. All I had to do was cross the street.

Not many people have lived in San Antonio as long as you have. Was your father in the military?

E: No, his first work was in a bank as a sort of financial officer. My uncle Izzy came to San Antonio because of the climate; he started a jewelry business and my parents came here to work with him. That business was the Alamo Jewelry Company, which closed within my lifetime. My cousins kept it up for years. That clock you see over there stood in the alcove outside the Alamo Jewelry Company. About 60 years ago someone called and said they were clearing out the basement in the old building and this clock was down there in three parts, and they wanted to get rid of it. We sent our boys, Jack and Stuart, who were in high school, down there to get it.

WOW: WONDERFUL OLD WOMEN

Which schools did you attend in San Antonio?

E: I went to Mark Twain Jr. High and graduated from Thomas Jefferson High.

If I remember correctly, you went to college in California. I'm sure that was extraordinary for a Texan in those days! Even today most Texans think UT Austin is as good as any university in America! Tell us how and why you went to college in California.

E: Things were different then. I knew I didn't want to stay in Texas because it wasn't well known as a place to learn. The whole idea for women was go to college and find a husband. I really was scholarly all my life. One of my high school teachers had gone to Mills College, a woman's college in Oakland, for a summer course. She told me Mills had an open competition for 20 merit scholarships. She convinced me to take the tests and I got in. Mills had a lot of foreign students from all over the world. I think they thought Texas was a foreign place! I attended Mills College for only one year though. There were well known professors there, including a famous dancer from Germany, who was the director of the dance department. I was always taking dance classes; dance was my minor. I had two sisters living in southern California at the time but the train took all day to get there. My mother thought it would be nice for me to be where I could visit my sisters frequently, so I transferred from Mills to UCLA. I went there for two years. It was hard and the professors were very demanding, but it was interesting. Jackie Robinson was in one of my classes. UCLA offered a different kind of exposure. The students in the arts programs put on a huge performance every year for the entire community. The performance incorporated music, art, costume and dance. We had to create our own choreography, costumes, everything. It was a fantastic experience. All my life when I go to concerts, if I hear certain music, I remember what I did to it. It was a very liberal and energizing experience.

Were the arts your focus at UCLA?

E: My main focus was always English literature. I was exposed to books I'd never heard of. The curriculum included nothing American—just British literature. I had to learn English history, which I'd never studied. The curriculum went all the way back to <u>Beowulf</u>, and the requirements included Old English as well as Middle English. That's when I changed my major because I didn't want to spend my time learning Old English. What would I ever do with that? For my senior year I attended UCBerkeley. I attended three very different but wonderful educational institutions.

When did you come back to San Antonio?

E: In 1941 when I graduated. Harold was waiting for me because he knew I wanted to finish college; we married that same year. I did meet another fellow while I was in college at Berkeley. My husband and he got to meet each other at my graduation. He was a very interesting young man, and I was very much in love with him. I do believe you can love two people at the same time. I would have probably been living in Shanghai now if I'd married him. He was born in Manchuria and his parents were White Russian. When the Czar took over, his folks had to flee and they went to Manchuria where he was born, and later they got into Shanghai. He went on to Stanford after Berkeley and for a while I had planned to go as well, but didn't because I got married. Many, many years later a friend from San Antonio met him at a party in Florida, and he asked if she knew me and proceeded to tell her the story of our time together. When she returned, she said, "I didn't know you were such a heartbreaker!"

How many years were you and Harold married?

E: If Harold had lived three more weeks, we would have been married 74 years. We had lots of fun together and a very good marriage.

What kind of fun things did you do?

E: Mostly travel. He loved Mexico and was fluent in Spanish and wanted our children to speak Spanish. We traveled a lot in Mexico. For many years, he and I drove to Rio Caliente, a spa near Guadalajara. There were hot spring pools, yoga, and excellent vegetarian food, which they grew in their own gardens. Harold would lead walks in the woods and I taught yoga and water aerobics. Harold had a lot of talents. Among other things, he was very good at math. Not too many years ago when our oldest grandson was working for Harold at the Monterrey Iron and Metal plant, he took out his calculator to figure out something. Harold grabbed it from him and said, "Do it in your head!" He was afraid kids depended on machines instead of their brains.

Did you and Harold travel other places?

E: Oh yes. For example, we went to Morocco three times and bought many Moroccan rugs. We had a friend who traveled with us who knew Morocco very well. The first trip we took to Morocco was a Smithsonian tour; it was a flop, because it was their first trip there. When we got back, our friend said, "You didn't see the real Morocco. Next year you're coming with me" and so we did. We learned a lot that trip.

Were you a stay at home mom when your three children were young?

E: I was a stay at home mom who worked. I helped at the store. Other members of my family owned Southern Music and Southern Jewelry. I worked during Christmas when they needed people to wrap packages or to take diamonds to the diamond setters. I was a go-for.

Didn't you also get a graduate degree at Trinity?

E: Yes, in Urban Studies. Before that I'd been doing a lot of work in the community as a volunteer. I'd been taking classes all along. I took classes occasionally at St Mary's University and San Antonio College. When our kids went to college, I went to college. I waited for them to leave. When they opened the department of Urban Studies at Trinity I went for an interview and the director was impressed by all the work I'd done in the community. I remember he told his secretary, "Close the door—don't let this woman get away!"

You've worked for so many organizations.

E: Yes, I think about 25. My daughter, Jill, made a list one time. Many Jewish women work only for Jewish organizations, but I didn't want to be limited to that. First I got on the Community Welfare Council, which is now United Way. Through that I got acquainted with many other organizations. In those days you really worked, you weren't just a name on a piece of paper. When I got out of college and came here the first organization that really put me to work was the American Association of University Women. That organization was never a big thing here, but they did important work in those days. They tested underprivileged or neglected children to determine their needs and where they belonged in school. I hadn't taken any psychology, so I was turned over to a psychiatrist who taught me the ropes.

Weren't you the first woman to head the Jewish Federation here?

E: Yes. Another woman started it, but she was never elected; when they began elections, it was all men until I was elected. I'll tell you an interesting story about that. Once when I went to the national meeting of presidents of Jewish Federations across the country, the man at the door directed me down the hall where the wives were meeting. I told him I was the president and he laughed. It was very demeaning. I had to force my way into the room. I was so unhappy I almost turned around and came home. That was the early 60s. Before that, we didn't have a Jewish Family Services. Despite the perceptions of some of the affluent Jews in the city, we found out that there were Jewish people in the community who had unmet needs and we hadn't been taking care of them. It took a long time for me to convince the board that we needed Jewish Family Services.

Was there one organization that you enjoyed working for more than others?

E: The National Council of Jewish Women. I worked locally and in the region and then got on the national board. They did so many wonderful things. I volunteered and they wanted to hire me at one point, but that would have required me to live part-time in Washington. Although I wasn't ready to commit to that, I did a lot of traveling usually with a black or Latina woman. I was invited to work at a professional level at the U.S. State Department.

Do you remember any discrimination against these non-white women when you travelled?

E: No, but I do remember discrimination when our family stayed at a hotel in Houston. Harold and I arranged for a babysitter for our kids while we went to dinner. I remember that when they went to dinner the babysitter who was black had to go down on the freight elevator while our kids took the normal elevator. We really raised Cain and found out it was a Texas Hotel Association rule that blacks had to take the freight elevators. This was a lovely and educated girl. Harold and I raised a lot of fuss about that. It was the same here. At the Majestic Theater the blacks had to sit upstairs and that's where our kids would sit. There were separate water fountains. Those kinds of things affected my developing sense of ethics. Not all the Jews in the community agreed with me, but I always think of that line in the Torah about remembering when we were strangers in Egypt and to behave accordingly.

Was it when you went to college in California that your eyes really opened to social injustice?

E: No, when I was younger I had travelled with my mother and sisters and we lived in California for two years when I was in Junior High. One of my best friends there was a black girl. I learned Japanese from the gardeners and made Japanese friends. It didn't occur to me that it was strange to have Japanese friends. We were brought up to think people were people. I learned a lot during those two years. Texas was certainly more provincial than California, but I have sweet memories of my school years here too. When I returned to San Antonio, I used to walk to school every day with my cousin and on the way home we'd stop and get a sour pickle. Right across the street from the school was a little concession where kids could get ice cream cones and sweets, but we always got pickles. I still love them!

Among your many accomplishments is a profound dedication to yoga. In fact, the Express-News called you the Mother of Yoga in the city. How did that begin?

E: We were in Mexico City when I was around 50, and friends were taking yoga classes; I'd never seen yoga before. When I got home there wasn't a yoga teacher in all of San Antonio, so I bought a book. Soon I was teaching my first yoga classes at the Healy Murphy learning center, a school for drop outs and also right here in my living room. At the Healy Murphy, I was applying what I had learned in my Urban Studies classes; for instance, I took the kids around town to the museums and other places they'd never been to. One funny thing happened: when I took them to the Police Department, the kids introduced me to the police, whom they knew, because they'd been arrested! I took them on a bus to Austin to see the Alvin Ailey dance troupe. Some of the kids even participated in a master class there. On the bus, one of the boys kept reaching in his pocket and of course the first thing I thought was "I wonder if he has a weapon." Finally he pulled out a big comb and I was so ashamed that I had been suspicious.

Didn't you also invite these troubled young people into your house and years later one of them called and told you what an impact that had on her life?

E: It wasn't over the phone. When Harold was in the hospital, one of the nurses' aides came up to me and told me that because I hadn't followed them around when they visited my home to make sure they weren't stealing, I had changed her life through my trust. She also reminded me that I'd told them to make their own paths, that just because other people in their family had made bad choices, they didn't have to. Another time a beautifully dressed girl came up to me and said that she'd been one of those students and she was now a lawyer. It was a program that changed lives.

So you were 50 when you started teaching yoga and taught here your house?

E: First I taught at Healy Murphy and then I had classes here. I still run into people who say they first did yoga on my floor! I also meet people who tell me their grandmother took yoga from me.

Are you still teaching yoga?

E: I have one class but it's out for the summer. I say I do mouth yoga now. I go to the class and help the teacher by talking or directing the students verbally. I still go to the League of Women Voters and SA 2020. I try to keep up with what's going on. I still go to daytime things. Sometimes I go out to lunch but it's hard for me to hear so I try to have people over here.

Have your attitudes about women and their roles changed over the years?

E: No. I've always felt we can do more and be more accepted in the work place and get paid better. Things have improved a little for women, but not enough.

What do you think shaped your life?

E: Marriage first. I had a wonderful husband. I didn't realize how many people appreciated Harold. I thought there wouldn't be many people at his funeral, because there aren't many people our age left. He was 100 and a half when he died! His fingers touched so many lives. In fact there were over 500 people at his funeral. He was such a special boss that people working in our business are now third generation. It's important to make younger friends, as we get older. Harold and I lost so many friends. Marriage and children came first, but over the years, yoga became a way of life for me. I learned to appreciate the connection between body, mind and spirit. And my Judaic studies made me aware of my own spirituality. I believe there are many spiritual paths, all leading to the same destination: a good life with kindness and respect for others.

The first yoga teaching school in San Antonio is named after you: The Esther Vexler Yoga Teaching School.

E: Yes, it's a little embarrassing, but nice. We just graduated our 5th group of teachers.

Did you ever think you'd live to be 97?

E: Never in a million years! All my sisters and brothers died before their 80s. My sister who lived the longest died at 75. I lost several siblings very young. One of my sisters died after her second child was born.

Do you think your longevity is because of your years of yoga?

E: I used to, but Harold would always say, "I don't do yoga" and he lived to be 100! We became quasi- vegetarians almost 50 years ago; maybe that helped us.

Were you a strict mother?

E: I was a worried mother. My son teases me when I worry about my grandchildren; he reminds me, "You know how you are." So with all the changes you make, some things never change.

Betty Ann Cody says she "waked up" at fifty, pursued a master's in counseling, and began her own counseling career; at 88, she still has clients, works out at a gym five or six days a week, and says that she has never been happier. Her home, which contains family heirlooms and photos, reflects her love of the color blue; she herself painted the back wall of her garage a dazzling turquoise so that she would feel joyful every time she arrived home.

BETTY ANNE CODY

BA: I decided that if you want to know me, you need to look at my home so I'm going to take you on a quick tour before we sit down. I'd like you to see what's important to me. This plate, for instance, belonged to my grandmother and it dates back to the Civil War. My grandmother was from Social Circle, Georgia, near Atlanta. She came from Georgia to East Texas where she met my grandfather. After they were married, they lived in Nacogdoches. That's where my mother grew up. This dining table was in my childhood home. It opens up and seats 12. I can remember playing under there and untying grown-ups' shoes. This cabinet was in my dad's house when he was a child and I use it to put all my pretties in. I really treasure it. Now, we'll go to the den.

Wow, you like blue!

BA: Yes, I do. It's beautiful and calm, and I love my yard. I went back there this morning and did a lot of trimming because it's grown so much with all the rain we've had. I don't get on ladders but I can reach pretty high. Over there, above the fireplace is a painting I love. I had always wanted a seascape and finally bought that one and had it shipped here from California. See this painting? I took each of my grandchildren on a glorious trip like to Greece, Alaska, the Caribbean, Paris. I asked my youngest when he was 16 and I was 80. I thought, "I need to take him now because later I may not be able to." It turned out to be a very wise thing because being responsible for a teenager is hard work. When he said he wanted to go to Greece, I asked him why, and he said he'd been studying Greece and world history and loved the myths. Then he added, "Neenie, you know that picture above your fireplace? Isn't that Greece? I've been looking at that all my life."

You never know what will grab a kid.

BA: You better be careful what you put out for them to see! That painting over there was painted for me when we lived in Kentucky. My husband was student minister and we lived on a college campus. One of the female students wanted to give us a gift; I told her when I was young I had a sailboat, so she painted that. That would've been in 1949. I just love it. This is the crosspiece from that family sailboat and the cap is a modern day imitation of the real cap we wore as children.

So where did you grow up?

BA: In Houston but we had a bay house on Galveston Bay and we moved there as soon as school was out and didn't move back until school started. We spent all our summers there. It was an idyllic childhood. Nobody had to report to anybody. We went home for meals and that was about it.

Were you allowed to sail on your own?

BA: No. That was too big a boat. I couldn't control it by myself. My brother and my daddy could sail it, and I was always begging them to take me sailing. So, that's my house. We'll go through the kitchen and back to the living room.

I love all the photos and sayings on your refrigerator.

BA: Yes, this one is my favorite - "I plan to live forever--so far, so good." And this cartoon- - "I'm livin' the dream"-- because that's what I'm doing. And I know it.

You were right. By looking around your house we got to see who you are. What fun. So, you grew up in Houston. Where did you meet your husband?

BA: At Baylor. We both went to Baylor in Waco, TX in '43 and were married in '47. I was pre-med for about 2 years and then I hit some of those high level physics and chemistry courses and I said I don't want to do that. About that time I met my husband so I had a real good reason to drop pre-med. After that, I majored in Bible, Biology and English lit.

What was Baylor like then?

BA: There were less than a thousand students. It was during WWII and it was a small campus. Everybody knew everybody. Small classes, 25-30 maximum.

Was it more religiously conservative than now?

BA: Yes, it was. No dancing. But we could have music. The school is much larger now.

Were you the first person in your family to go to college?

BA: No, no. My mother and father both went to college. My dad had an MD from Vanderbilt and came back and practiced in Houston as an anesthesiologist. My mom was a music major. She said she wanted to get a job, but my father said, "If you want everybody in town to think I can't support you and my family, then you go ahead and get a job." That's the way it was in those days.

Did your husband have the same ideas about your working?

BA: No. I really had three careers. First, child rearing, then helping him with his work, and the third was counseling. I went back to school here at Our Lady of the Lake and got a master's degree in counseling and opened up a counseling business at 54.

I know you also have a deep interest in music. When did that begin?

BA: When I was an infant! My mother and a friend were taking singing lessons together in Houston and they would bring me and the other woman's baby with them. We babies would lie on the floor and listen to our mothers singing. While I was growing up, my mother listened to the Metropolitan Opera broadcasts every Saturday afternoon on the radio, and I often listened with her. She and I also loved to sing together in harmony. Once when I was in fourth grade when my school class was singing "God Bless America," I started singing in harmony. When the teacher asked, "Who is singing in harmony?" I thought I was in trouble. But just the opposite: she said, "Keep singing! You have a wonderful gift!" That was an important affirmation for me and I did keep singing.

Where and when did you sing?

BA: When I was a student at Baylor, I sang in the largest choir. When Bill and I moved to Fort Worth where he earned his master's degree I took my first voice lessons and was accepted into the touring choir along with a close friend. She and I had to work hard to catch up with the rest of the choir members who had been working on the material before we were accepted to join as alto singers. I also studied voice with the director. When we moved to Kentucky I organized and directed the Baptist Student Union Choir and toured with thirty students in small towns all over Kentucky. At the

Baptist Student Union Convention in North Carolina we performed before 3,000 people! Over the years, wherever we moved, I was singing or directing choirs or both. I performed solo portions of Messiah in Nashville, and later was an alto soloist in Richmond, Virginia, where I was paid for singing for the first time. While in Richmond I also served as the interim director of the choir in the Richmond Choral Society and we sang Elijah, Messiah, and Distler's Oratorio. Since living in San Antonio I've sung with many choirs including at Christ Episcopal Church where I was employed to organize the pastoral care. With that church I toured England; with the First Presbyterian Church choir, I toured Budapest, Vienna, and Salzburg.

How wonderful to do what you love and see the world at the same time! Do your children sing?

BA: My daughter Kathy and I both sang with the Texas Bach Choir and St. Luke's Choir. She has a piano degree from UT Austin.

Perfect! You sang as a child with your mother and later as a mother with your own child! Do you still sing now?

BA: Because of physical problems, I can't sing well anymore. However, a friend told me she read that singing strengthens the brain; so every day I stand up and sing old hymns for ten minutes. So there it is: singing helps my brain, body and soul all at the same time.

Please tell us about the early years of your marriage.

BA: My husband's work was first with the Baptist Church on the University of Kentucky campus. Then in Nashville with the Southern Baptist Headquarters working with the national office of Baptist students. Our son and daughter were born there. His work involved a lot of travel. Then he moved to the International Mission Board in Richmond, VA. After that, he came back to Dallas and worked for Howard Butt organizing Christian leadership conferences. And from there we moved to San Antonio and then to the retreat center outside Leakey, Texas, on the Frio River. He retired in 1979 and we moved back here.

How many years did you live at the retreat center?

BA: We lived there in a beautiful house for 7 years. We rented out this house we're talking in during that time. Our kids were grown and gone, so it was just the two of us.

Were you brought up in a religious environment?

BA: Yes. Our family attended church regularly and my mother was a leader there. I was a third generation Baylor student which at the time was a very religious institution run by the Baptist church.

Did your counseling career begin after your husband died?

BA: No, my husband died in 1995. I got my master's degree years before that in '81 and I started working on the staff of Christ Episcopal Church in '82 and worked there for 6 years. Then I opened an office of my own in '88.

Does your counseling have a blend of religion?

BA: It depends on the client. Religious counseling is called pastoral care or pastoral counseling. It's what they call Christian counseling. I am not a Christian counselor. I am a Christian who is a counselor. I don't lay anything on my clients. They know who I am when they come, so they can figure it out. When the industry of mental health insurance began about 25 years ago, all of us in our group said we'd just get on all the lists. That allowed us to have a real cross-section of people from the various local businesses that sent their employees to us and we had a huge variety.

Do you have a specialty?

BA: I prefer to work with women.

Is that because some men might find you too forceful?

BA: Yes. Definitely. Because I am forceful. I tell it like it is. I took some special training to work with couples and enjoyed that very much. Adults only. No teenagers or children. That requires a whole different training.

You still see patients right here in your living room?

BA: Yes, this past Wednesday I saw three clients here.

Do you know any other counselors your age who still see clients?

BA: No, I don't.

D: How old are you now?

BA: I'm 88.

At 88 you are so different from what most people have in their minds as the typical 88 year old.

BA: Well, that's changed a lot in the past 20 years. People take better care of themselves and eat better. You don't have to dread being 80 like we used to.

What I'm getting from you is that your life hasn't changed that much because of your age.

BA: I'm slower. I make better choices. I don't climb on ladders. I think that for older people the "f" word is fall.

As the years passed, did you think I'm not going to get old, or have you just been living and not really contemplating getting older?

BA: Both of those attitudes. My daughter asked me recently when I started going to the gym and I realized that in 1990 a friend invited me to go on a sailing trip off of Florida. We were to sail out and see and swim with the dolphins, and I thought I needed to get myself in shape. So when I was 63 I began going to the gym and got a trainer. She got me swimming. As it turns out, we couldn't swim in the Atlantic on that trip because of the storms. It was so stormy that we had to walk on our knees on the boat and I came home bruised all over. It was wonderful and I would do it again! So now I go 6 days a week for 30-45 minutes. I ride a recumbent bicycle. The least I do is 20 minutes on the bicycle. The most is 30 minutes on the bicycle and then I do arm and leg strengthening. I also have a trainer twice a week.

You are probably her prized pupil.

BA: I am!

Do people look at you and think wow!

BA: Last week I was working out and as I went from one machine to another a gentleman stopped me and told me how inspired everyone was by my working out.

Do you feel stronger?

BA: Of course.

Did you ever feel frail?

BA: No. I've always exercised. Years ago I was a tennis player. My mother played tennis.

Was your mother unusual for her generation?

BA: My mother was, and so was my grandmother.

But they were southern ladies!

BA: My grandmother lived in Nacogdoches. She married Mr. Dotson and always called him Mr. Dotson. He had been a drummer boy in the Confederate Army, was captured and taken prisoner; when the war was over and he was released, he walked all the way home to Atlanta. They all did. My grandmother was very much a Confederate woman. She taught herself Shakespeare and had a complete collection of his work. I knew her in her 60s and I thought she was terribly old, of course! I loved to go and see her. She was a big, big Baptist but she played cards and she said she knew God forgave her because she didn't have that much else to do. Isn't that something? She didn't go to college but all of her children graduated from Baylor. My dad grew up in Abilene. He finished Baylor and went to medical school at Vanderbilt.

I'm still intrigued by these southern women who aren't the typical frail, vaporish women from the south.

BA: There's not a one in my crowd. My aunt was a radio actress in New York. Her husband worked for Thomas Edison when he was selling Victrolas.

I know that you are very politically progressive. Growing up in the south, what were your family's attitudes toward African Americans?

BA: We had a black maid full time. She came at 7a.m. and left after the dinner dishes were done. She was my nanny and also did everything else. She cooked. She cleaned. None of us knew or asked about her own family, which she also had to care for.

What did you call her?

BA: I called her Annie. I never knew her last name, but my mother did. When social security came in, Mother took her down and got her signed up.

How did your family feel about integration?

BA: Did you see the movie "The Help"? That is accurate to a T. The main thing I recall from my childhood is seeing that when two black people were waiting for a bus they spoke as if they knew each other. I took that to mean they took care of each other, whether they knew each other or not. My mother occasionally took me down to the 9th ward in Houston to donate clothing and other things. At Baylor some of us did volunteer work in the slums surrounding the campus where there were pathetic shacks. That's the way things were, and very few people spoke up and said, "This isn't the way it should be." There was no sense of injustice.

How about in the church?

BA: That was worse. Many pastors who encouraged black people to join the church were fired immediately. I had some friends who lost their jobs.

Has the church changed in a positive way?

BA: Yes, both the Baptist and Episcopal. I moved from the Baptist church to the Episcopal Church. We have several black members now.

Why did you switch from Baptist to Episcopal?

BA: When we were at Laity Lodge many faiths came. It was ecumenical so we met many Episcopalians. When my husband retired, he decided to switch and asked if I wanted to, and I was also ready to change.

Was there backlash?

BA: Oh yes.

How do you view religion? Does it matter to you what denomination you are?

BA: No, it does not. It matters to me who I am. I care about who you are and what you believe, but I'm not going to try to convince you to believe what I do. If you ask, I'll tell you what I believe, but not otherwise. I'm changing what I believe as time goes by. I now believe in a God of mercy and love. Spirituality is central to my life. I have taken classes at the Oblate School of Theology here in San Antonio.

Other than religion, what are your interests?

BA: I love to read. I watch TV and movies. I'm pretty choosey though. I'm with friends a lot. I go to lunch a lot. And, of course, the gym.

So your friends are still around?

BA: Yes, some, but recently I went to two funerals in 4 weeks. What I do is make time to be with the friends who are left. We are together as much as possible.

Do you cultivate younger friends?

BA: I try. But it's not easy.

Talk a bit about your marriage.

BA: Well, I was a good, traditional wife until I finally waked up and realized I needed to take care of myself. My husband had health issues and I finally realized that if he died, I wouldn't have anything. No income, nothing. I didn't want to depend on my children. And so I went to school, not knowing if I could do it or not. But on the first exam when I got an A I knew I could do it. When I opened the mail, I stood at my front door and just bounced up and down! I finished with a 3.8 GPA, a master's degree and licensure as a psychotherapist.

By your description, you changed from being a pretty docile woman and wife to a strong, mature woman.

BA: That took years and lots of work.

It's interesting that you really came into your own in your 50s. Looking at you now, it's hard to believe that you were ever a little wife.

BA: We met at 16 and married at 20. We didn't really know each other. I had a lot of growing up to do.

Do you think your parents brought you up to be strong?

BA: No. I don't think that's true. They brought me up to be a good little girl. I taught myself to be strong when I waked up at 50.

Have your interests changed over the years?

BA: Yes. I'm interested in more things and do more things. I've taken some wonderful trips. I've taken my grandchildren, each one alone, on big trips. I went with a friend to study at the Jungian psychology center in Switzerland. I'm not a Jungian counselor, but I include some of what I ingested of that body of thought.

I want to go back to your awakening.

BA: I was slow claiming that I'm a person and that I matter just as much as anyone. This was brand new for me as well as for my husband. It was very hard to adjust to. For both of us. All of this was during the time of the women's movement. The whole thing fits together.

What do you think of the fact that many women are still fighting the same battles now?

BA: I'm very sad about women who don't stand up for themselves. It's largely conservative Christians.

Are there things that shock you in the world? Are there issues that you thought would be resolved by now?

BA: I used to believe in the war to end all wars. I thought this has been so awful, hundreds of thousands of people killed, it won't happen again. Now I know we will always be fighting somewhere.

Do you think that's human nature?

BA: Can you think of a time there weren't wars? And now in Texas you can carry a pistol everywhere.

Do you give words of wisdom to your kids?

BA: If they ask. I learned this. You don't give uninvited advice because it's mostly taken as criticism. I do not advise my kids. I really don't. I can't know what they are supposed to do. These are different times; I cannot know what my grandchild should do.

In a marriage when one person makes a big shift, it's hard. Did the two of you ever consider separating?

BA: No, we did not. We had a basic commitment to the marriage.

So to you divorce wasn't a choice.

BA: No. Neither of us wanted that. Our love for each other endured the trials.

What do you think you've figured out by now?

BA: A lot. I figured out it's a good thing to be alive and have fun. I've never had as much fun as I do now. I'm the happiest I've ever been.

What sustains you?

BA: Friendships. Family. Music. Daily prayer. I don't study scripture a whole lot but I do sometimes. If I come across something I don't understand, I just skip it.

Would you have done that when you were younger?

BA: No. I would've taken it literally.

What do you give yourself permission to do now that maybe you didn't when you were younger?

BA: Well, almost anything. My toenails are turquoise, my favorite color. One of the things I've learned is I'm not ashamed anymore. If I've committed a sin, I've given it to God and He's taken care of it. I'm not walking around carrying shame or guilt.

Was that part of the waking up?

BA: Yes. My waking up is knowing that I am a person who is important. I know now that we are all doing the best we can. I don't need to criticize people because I don't know what they are grappling with and they don't know my story either.

What takes away your energy? What do you dread?

BA: If people suck the life out of me, I don't spend time with them. I can't help them. When I was younger, I wouldn't have done that. That's why I had headaches and other ailments. Pain is a gift. It tells you that you need to pay attention to what's going on in your life.

How about retiring?

A: I've retired 4 times and just came back. It was always because someone asked me to do something, told me they needed me. I've got 4 regular clients now; we meet here in my living room.

When your husband died, did you know how to take care of your finances? Was that part of your waking up?

BA: While he was still alive I knew I needed to be financially responsible. I have continued that. I live debt-free now.

Did you ever have a mentor?

BA: I don't think I had an ongoing mentor except Madeleine L'Engle, a woman who stayed with us a lot. She was a speaker at Laity Lodge. She was a well -known author; she died a few years ago at 88. She was from New York, had written all her life, and travelled all over speaking. She wrote every day. She looked at me and communicated to me that I was a whole person. Not many people had ever done that before, and it helped me grow and it's still a surprise. She was as close to a mentor as I've ever had. And we played the most amazing ping-pong!

Do you think the idea of wholeness is unique to women?

BA: I hope not. It's an awareness that most people don't have or think about. I think a great percentage of women in our culture don't see themselves as very important. That's why they vote against women's rights. Most women haven't waked up. They have strong husbands and other influences that keep them from claiming who they are.

Do you dream?

BA: Sometimes I recall my dreams. There was a time that I remembered and recorded them and was even in a group where we discussed them.

Do you have a daily routine?

BA: No. Each day is whatever I want it to be.

Does anything get under your skin?

BA: Very little bothers me. Things that used to bother me just don't matter that much anymore.

What makes you happiest?

BA: Being with my family. I'm so happy about who they are. They are good people and married good people and have good children. I led a book group recently about a book that required us to write down 300 things we are grateful for. My notebook had 363 things I'm grateful for. I'm thankful for the color of this room, the sheets on the bed, the rug on the floor, the shoes on my feet and the turquoise on my toes! Listening to music! Jazz, classical, country, all of it!

Was gratitude something you knew when you were younger?

BA: I learned it more as I got older and I believe it is vital.

What do you want people to know about you?

BA: I'm a lover, not a fighter. I love to study, to learn, to grow in spirit and wisdom. I love life.

Gifted pianist and educator, Mary Esther Bernal, taught public school for many years and incorporated music into her entire curriculum. Her classes were so popular that for several years none of her students missed even one day of class. For decades she was the volunteer pianist and organist at San Fernando Cathedral. One year at the Cathedral, she directed seven different choirs. She is now one of "The Divas," a local political advisory committee that vets candidates and encourages reform; she remains active in the community, organizes foreign travel trips for friends, and continues to use her musical gift playing piano at a retirement home.

MARY ESTHER BERNAL

Before we go any further, please tell us about the photo we just saw on the wall of you and Pope John Paul II.

ME: The Pope was here in San Antonio in 1987 and of course he visited San Fernando Cathedral, the center of the Catholic Church in the city. My choir was upstairs in the choir loft and we were the only lay people there other than the ushers. My choir got to sing a song as the Pope entered. They sang a song from Our Lady of Guadalupe called "Ante Tu Altar." He loved the song and we sang it again as he exited the Cathedral. Several years later, during my (and Joe's) visit to Rome in 1993, San Antonio Archbishop Patrick Flores asked Joe and me to deliver a letter to the Swiss Guard at the Vatican, and the next day we were asked to visit the Pope in his chapel at the Vatican. The letter sent by the Archbishop was an introduction of me as the Director of Music at the San Fernando Cathedral. After giving us Communion, he met with us in his dining room and presented each of us with a rosary. He told us of his fond memories of San Antonio and how he enjoyed hearing the choir sing the song to the Virgen de Guadalupe!

You were the director of music at San Fernando Cathedral?

ME: Yes. For 32 -35 years. I've always been so appreciative to God for giving me a musical gift that I never accepted payment for my organ and choir work at the cathedral. The choir accepted donations when we would play and sing at weddings and special occasions, and that money was used for our annual banquet.

Are you a San Antonio native?

ME: I was born March 21, 1935 at Santa Rosa Hospital, and my family lived on the South side. My dad always had a piano and his mom (voice) and dad (violin) were talented in music. As I grew older, I could always pick out the songs "by ear" like my father.

You mean you could simply hear a song and then play it?

ME: Yes. And this was when I was real little, even before I went to school. My father would play a song with one finger; if he hit a wrong note, I would say, "It hurts my ears." I had a wonderful teacher, Sister Vivian, when I began school at St. Leo's and my dad requested that she teach me piano. When I was 5 1/2 the nun would play a song and I would play it back for her. I have a very good ear. What I didn't learn on paper, I could play once I heard it. From this early age, I would accompany all the musical programs at school on the piano. This included choir, soloists, and special programs.

Do you still have the ability to listen to something and then play it?

ME: I'm even better now and I've added a little jazz, Mexican songs, and other styles and cultures to my classical repertoire. Anyway, I always went to Catholic schools, and the nuns had me playing the piano and then the organ. I think that's why I don't have any problems with my feet or hands because I've always kept them moving. You know with the organ you have to play the pedals as well as the keyboard. One day the music and theater teacher from Fox Tech High School heard me play and invited me to play the piano for a musical they were performing at the school. This led me into accompanying in Little Theater and musicals in the community. One major development happened while I was a student at St. Henry's Academy, the high school I graduated from in 1952. A lady from the King Ranch heard me play and told the nun who was the music teacher at my high school that I needed to go to college. Up until then my goal was to graduate from St. Henry's Academy and then go and apply for a salesperson's position at Joske's of Texas Department Store in downtown San Antonio.

Your goal wasn't musical?

ME: I absolutely loved music, but it wasn't my lifetime goal. I always loved to play at any occasion, mostly extracurricular activities. Anyway, the lady from King Ranch notified my teacher that she was giving me a scholarship when I graduated high school, and so I enrolled at Our Lady of the Lake College in 1952. I sent the lady a thank you note, but I never saw her again or really knew her. I graduated in 1952 and entered a four- year degree program in piano. I was so lucky to have such great teachers at Our Lady of the

Lake. I had one nun in particular, Sister Elaine, who had perfect pitch and was a great inspiration to me. I don't have perfect pitch, but I have relative pitch and always strived for perfect pitch. For instance, I can tell my piano is out of tune today with all this wet weather we've had. I learned Mozart and Beethoven and Chopin and many, many more. I remember telling the nun I could improve on Mozart!

Really? How? That's a great line!

ME: Mozart had such beautiful technical skill but some of his melodies didn't seem to properly follow the drama of some of his music. Beethoven was big and dramatic and I loved it. But I loved melodious music as well. When I did shows, sometimes I would improvise, adding a little Mozart here, some Beethoven here, and a few Mexican songs here and there! Teachers loved me because I could take a piece and make it bigger.

Do you write music?

ME: Not really. I just improvise and arrange. I did write the school song for one of the elementary schools where I taught. It was a big hit! One of my grandsons is a singer, and he's my own Andrea Bocelli. He graduated from Texas State University this year with a degree in Music Theater and Opera. Presently he's performing in Connecticut. The oldest grandson is a marine sergeant and in the United States Marine traveling band. He's the one who has perfect pitch and plays trumpet and keyboards. While at Chatsworth High School in Los Angeles he played with the Pasadena Symphony and when he was a senior he was the drum major for the student band in the New Year's Day parade in Pasadena.

You obviously passed along your musical talents. Did you also inherit them?

ME: Yes, my grandmother had an operatic voice, but never performed. They were very poor and came up from Mexico. My father inherited a lot of interest in music from her and played the piano. My mother sang beautifully and on pitch but she never studied. She had 9 siblings and they moved here from Eagle Pass. My father had one brother and his father played the violin and was in a little combo with all string instruments. My grandparents lived with us until they died. My dad passed away in the 50s and my mom lived with our family until she passed away.

When did you meet your husband?

ME: I met Joe Juarez Bernal when I was a senior at Our Lady of the Lake. He was a teacher with the San Antonio Independent School District (SAISD). We married in 1956 and celebrated our 59th anniversary this year. I never tell anyone how old I am, but if I tell people how long I've been married, it gives it away!

Is your husband musical like you?

ME: No, but he loves music and loves to dance. His father, his brothers and Joe all loved to play ball. His father died when he was only 42 years old and left his mother with nine children. She did get a small pension from the railroad where he worked. She was always very proud to say that five of her sons were in the United States military service at the same time, and they all survived service in the war. We both come from very poor families with middle class values. We were taught to appreciate school and learning and we also learned English and Spanish.

So did you earn your living musically?

ME: No. I taught school for 32 years. I began teaching in 1958 as a regular elementary classroom teacher. In 1972 I was named Director of Cultural Arts, and in 1977 I was named Director of Bilingual Education for San Antonio Independent School District, which at the time was the largest school district in San Antonio. In 1988, until I retired in 1993, I was the Director of Arts and Languages. After I retired there was a vacancy on the SAISD Board of education. I ran for the position and I won the election, serving from 1996 to 2004. As for the services at San Fernando Cathedral I volunteered my services, the major choir being a Latin Choir that sang at the Sunday High Mass and was well recognized in the city. One year I had 7 choirs, including a children's choir, a seniors' choir, a youth choir and a mariachi choir. Joe and I got married in 1956 five days after I graduated from college. We had a traditional Mexican wedding. Our first little home was on West Avenue. He was already a teacher and had a nice salary of about $2,000 annually. And I started that year with the Cathedral. It's a very old Cathedral built in 1731, and the organ is from 1854. I sort of grew up there and so did my kids. Joe got into politics in 1964 and was elected as a State Representative and in 1966 he was elected as a State Senator. He retired from the Texas Senate in 1972. He was elected to the State Board of Education in 1994 and served for eight years. My degree was in music and my mother questioned what I would do with that degree, so I got my teacher certification and became a classroom teacher. I never taught music per se, because I didn't have the patience. I would have expected too much! When my talented grandson came along, I broke that rule and coached him.

Did you teach elementary school?

ME: Yes, with my degree in piano and organ and teacher and administrative certification I was qualified to teach elementary through high school. The elementary school hired me and I taught third grade and loved it. The principal placed a piano in my classroom and I incorporated music into the curriculum. I taught my Spanish-speaking students English by teaching them music. We had science songs and other instructional songs in most classes. I always followed the curriculum but included music. I had one class for two years, and none of them—or I-- ever missed a class! Amazing.

They probably couldn't wait to get to school!

ME: Even when I switched schools I continued to teach the curriculum using music. Later in the 60s and 70s that was a big thing and considered very innovative.

You certainly were ahead of your time!

ME: In 1965 they pulled me out of the classroom to focus on ESL.

What did you think about being a politician's wife?

ME: I loved it. We lived in Austin the first session when Joe was elected and our sons went to school there. While they were in school I'd go attend the sessions at the State Capitol and I really enjoyed all the politics. I'm proud to say that my husband passed important legislation while a legislator, which includes UTSA, the Medical school and the Dental School. He also passed the 45-minute planning for each classroom teacher in the state and the first Bilingual Education Act in Texas that allows teaching in a language other than English.

Did you ever think about going into politics yourself?

ME: Not until I retired from teaching when there was a vacancy on the school board. As I mentioned before, I ran in 2001, won and was on the board until 2004. After that I continued being involved in the community by being active in the retired teachers' organizations, and other groups like the Women's Hall of Fame and the Council of Presidents.

You must have tremendous energy to work full time, raise four children and also direct music at the Cathedral.

ME: My mother was around so that helped. My children were her only grandchildren and she loved to take care of all of them.

When you listen to music, what do you enjoy?

ME: I love listening to singers like Andrea Bocelli and opera.

Your grandmother influenced you?

ME: I think so. But the kind of music I've always heard is the old Mexican/Spanish music like "Granada." And the old love songs including the songs that the mariachis sing.

So you are retired now. Are you still active in education?

ME: I retired from the Cathedral when they changed the rector in the early 90s. I just had to leave even though I still enjoyed it. There were just so many other things I didn't have time for. I decided I'd do more community work. I've been working with some high schools on their scholarship programs. And we have a group of women who meet every Friday morning; I have dubbed us "The Divas." We have our table at Mi Tierra and we're treated very well. We've been meeting since 2006 and hardly miss a Friday. We invite people who are interested in running for office or who are in office to come and break "tacos" with us. We share ideas and talk about the issues of the day and future. We ask them about their best thinking on issues of our community, state and nation. If they are running for office, what are their goals and how do they plan to govern, if elected. We share our issues with them also.

You must be a group with considerable clout.

ME: All of the women in the group are "movers and shakers." We meet with the city department heads and police and fire chiefs. Our goal is to make sure they know what the important issues are. We share our views and encourage them. Most of us are a part of the San Antonio Women's Hall of Fame group. This is a statewide organization founded in 1984 that nominates women who have made contributions to the city--mainly women helping women. The women are chosen in sixteen categories. I'm involved in the local chapter and was president from 2004-2008.

How many grandchildren do you have?

ME: Six Bernal boys and one boy and one girl from my daughter-in-law who is married to our second son.

How do you incorporate music into your life now?

ME: I'm involved with a very heartwarming project. On Tuesdays I go to a retirement home where a friend works. I know some of the residents who live there also. They asked me to play the piano, and some of the residents came in to listen. This group now comes in every Tuesday for one hour and we sing together and once in a while we have a soloist and/or a duet. Many of the participants have Alzheimer's and yet, when I start a song they begin to sing and they know the words. Several are in wheel chairs and some use walkers. Some have retired there just because it is a beautiful place and the services are very good. They help the others find the words in our music notebook. We've named them "The Happy Singers." They have so much fun, and we all look forward to that time of the week. When I get there, they are all waiting for me. We've been together now for over two years and they have presented two patriotic programs, an Irish Program, two Christmas programs, a Thanksgiving program—with great attendance at each performance. The last one was a full house!

It's wonderful that you keep using your musical talent as a gift. Have you ever charged for playing music?

ME: On special occasions like weddings I charge, but I don't schedule that many anymore. Everything I do now is for family, friends, and other groups who volunteer as I do.

Since you love popular music as well as classical music, did you ever think of playing in a club?

ME: No, not really. I play when I'm invited. And I love it. The songbook I use for the Happy Singers is from The Landing on the Riverwalk. They're all sing-along popular songs. We supplement our notebook with other popular songs and choir member also bring us the words to other songs.

It's incredible how generously you've used your talent.

ME: Well, I had four children and a husband in politics. We really had to use our time wisely, but we're proud of our beautiful family and grateful for all the blessings we've received. Now we're enjoying our grandchildren.

What do you do in your off time?

ME: In the mornings I read the paper. I try to keep up with what's happening. Recently I started working with the Mexican American Unity Council Scholarship Fund. They do wonderful things in the community and give scholarships to students at a couple of local high schools. MAUC got two good grants and we focus on the students who have potential but may not have done exceptionally well in high school. The students who did really well will get other scholarships. We want the ones who didn't quite make it. And we require the recipients to do community work. We also work with them and teach them how prepare for interviews and in the job situations. We've even worked with a few homeless students and provided very necessary resources for them to go, and stay, in college.

You certainly give back to San Antonio.

ME: Well, it's just a matter of living isn't it? It makes us happy to be asked to help.

We love your house. It's so comfortable.

ME: We've been here since 1968 and love it. We have an acre of land so we've got plenty of room. I love to feed the birds. If I don't get out there in the morning to feed them, they get after me. We also have three big dogs. Next week I'm going over to join the "no kill" program.

You certainly keep active. You don't seem to be slowing down.

ME: I am slower than before because I want to enjoy my retirement. And, I have a couple of health issues, and allergies that get to me. This morning I felt bad because of the rain or the mold until I had my breakfast taco. Then I was fine!

You are a real San Antonio woman! What do you do for fun, when you just spend your time frivolously?

ME: Joe and I are Scrabble fiends. We read the Scrabble dictionary for a week before we play! Some of The Divas play. We invite other couples and have maybe 4 tables going at a time. Church is also a big part of our lives. My grandson sings in the choir at the church we go to. Our family gets together every Sunday. We have a potluck and barbecue out in the yard. If we don't feel like cooking, we go out. But the point is for all of us to get together each week. We also love to travel. We are planning a trip now and already have fifteen people signed up for it.

You mean you are organizing a group tour?

ME: That's another one of my pastimes. We've done it for about sixteen years now. We just got back from Germany a couple months ago. Next trip will be to Italy. A travel company contacted us years ago when we retired as teachers. At that time the focus was to get teachers in San Antonio to go on the trips. We've been to many countries and have returned to a few. We've been to the Vatican several times.

Was this the house where all the kids wanted to be when your children were growing up?

ME: Oh yes. All their friends would come here. Many still do!

You seem so energetic mentally and physically. Did you inherit that?

ME: My mother was a beautiful woman. She was so beautiful I was embarrassed that I was her daughter. She came to San Antonio in the '20s and was Miss Orchidia and her dress was made out of window drapes--a curtain-- because they had no money. She was the one who encouraged me to think about teaching school. She was proud of me! The only thing I regret is that my mother didn't teach me how to cook. She was a fabulous cook. But I was always playing the piano while everyone was cooking! Before you leave, I'll play a little Mozart and Beethoven for you. Did you know that "Amazing Grace" is played on only the black keys? I'll show that too.

P.S.

Driving home from your house, Mary Esther, I heard that President Obama ended his eulogy for the murdered black minister of the AME church in Charleston with a rendition of Amazing Grace. Had you heard about that when you played it for us yesterday?

ME: No. **Amazing grace** indeed.

Maxine Cohen lost family members in the Holocaust. In response to this family history, she read voluminously about that event and developed into a highly respected educator teaching about the Holocaust and stressing the importance of understanding how and why ordinary people became Nazis. For years she spearheaded the development of a center for teaching about the Holocaust. (www.jfsatx.org/what-we-do1/holocaust-memorial-museum-of-san-antonio) When her husband suffered a horrifying brain stem stroke, she hit bottom, but over the years she has become once again strong, vital, and resilient; she uses her lively sense of humor and unmistakable intelligence to support family members and social causes.

MAXINE COHEN

Let's start with your early life. What were your parents like?

MC: My mom was a housewife who never had the education she wanted and more than anything, she wanted her four children to have everything she had missed. My parents were extremely good with each other. That's a gift for children, by the way. They were really good friends. She was quiet and very pretty, but the world was not a comfortable place for her. We lived in Galion, a small town in Ohio, until I was fourteen. It was like a cocoon. She didn't have to reach out; she stayed very close to home. She died in her late 50s. My father was a wise and gentle man. He never said a harsh word to me that I can remember. He was quiet, but when he spoke to his children, we listened. No one argued with him, not his children and not the people who worked for him. They liked and respected him.

When did your family come to America?

MC: My mother and father were both born in Europe. They came to the United States before the quota system was adopted in the 1920s. They were young. My father emigrated several years before she did, probably at the age of 15 or 16. She was six years younger than he, and as far as I can figure out, came to this country when she was about fourteen or fifteen. They had Austrian passports, but the area they lived in became part of Poland after World War I. When my mother arrived in the States, she was met by her father who had come earlier with two of his older children. He sent for my mother. Within a year or two of her arrival, he returned to Europe intending to bring his wife and three younger children back to this country. Unfortunately, his plans didn't work out. Shortly after he returned to Europe in 1914, World War I began. He was conscripted into the Austrian army and served for four years. He was a very religious Jew; serving in the military must have been very hard for him. He never regained his health and he died a few years after he was released from the army. My mother and father were distant cousins. They didn't live in the same town in Europe, but she knew him. My mother's family was poor. My father's family was not wealthy, but they were comparatively comfortable. My paternal grandparents had 7 children I know about. Except for the youngest who stayed with his parents presumably to help with their business, my grandfather sent his children away as soon as they were old enough to travel alone. My father, the oldest, was the first to leave. He never saw his parents again. Altogether, five siblings came to the United States. Because of U.S. immigration restrictions, one brother later immigrated to Argentina.

In 1938 with reports of Nazi anti-Semitism growing more and more alarming, my mother and her sister Rose began the difficult process of filing for visas for their unmarried brother and sister. Rose was the driving force in the effort. Two visas were finally approved, but unfortunately, only the brother was permitted to enter the U.S. Chana, the sister, was sent back to Europe because she was ill. A few months later, Germany invaded Poland. World War II began and immigration was no longer a possibility. The uncle who was rescued came to live with us in Ohio.

Both my parents' families lived in the area of Poland that was occupied by the Soviet Union in 1939. When Nazi Germany invaded that area in 1941, my paternal grandfather was taken into hiding by a Christian neighbor. Both he and the neighbor were shot and killed. The other members of both families perished and it has been impossible to trace records of them.

What language did your uncle speak when he came to live with you?

MC: Yiddish, but he learned English very quickly. My parents spoke Yiddish to each other sometimes and to relatives, but they spoke only English to their children. Just a few years ago, my oldest sister told me her first language was Yiddish, but I was the fourth and youngest child. By the time I came along, their English was comfortable for them. In that small town in Ohio, Yiddish was rarely spoken by anyone even among the few Jewish friends they had.

Was there a synagogue in the small town?

MC: No. The nearest synagogue was in another town about 15 miles away. We went to Sunday school there, and very often, we went to Cleveland for the Jewish holidays. My parents had relatives there. I was the only Jewish kid in my school. The few other

Jewish children in town did not attend my neighborhood school. I didn't experience any anti- Semitism. My father was well respected, but being Jewish affected the rhythm of our lives. My parents weren't very observant, but there was always Shabbat and the Jewish holidays. There was never any question--we were different from the people in our neighborhood, but being different was not painful probably because our family ties were strong.

Were you an only child?

MC: I had three sisters, all considerably older than I. Sylvia was nearly 14 years older, Dorothy 12 years and Jeanette 8 years. They began to marry when I was barely in my teens. Two of them married men from Cleveland. We moved there a couple of years later. I never liked Cleveland and leaving Galion was a jolt. In school, I had been the top of my class and suddenly I was with students who were a lot more advanced than I was. I had wanted to move to a bigger town so I could take music lessons from a better teacher. I knew even then that living in a small town had disadvantages because the schools were not the best, but there is a sense of community and place in a small town. When we moved to_Cleveland, a big city, I was anonymous. Our house was smaller. The neighborhood was not as pretty. It was not a happy time for me.

Was music your first interest?

MC: Yes, but in hindsight it was a mistake. I wasn't a first rate talent. I played well and I loved the music, but it was probably not where I belonged. If I'd had counseling at home or at school, I might have taken a different route, probably history or literature. When I went to college I majored in music, which in retrospect was not a good path. If you are going to be a pianist, you need more physical talent than I had. I was good but not outstanding and I had other interests. When I look at my grandchildren and try to recall what I was like at their age, all I remember is confusion. I think with guidance I would have done something different, but my parents supported my musical ambitions, particularly my mother. She adored music and always dragged me to concerts.

When you graduated college, what did you do?

MC: I got married; that was the common path. I met him in college, but the marriage didn't last. He was a very good-looking guy from a wealthy family. We were divorced after a very short time._

Was your divorce a big shock in those days?

MC: My parents were Victorian, especially my mother, but they were very understanding. If they were worried, they kept it to themselves. They wanted me to be happy. In general, I think my parents were quite permissive, probably because I was the fourth child. They always expected us to do the right thing. For example, never once did either of them ask me if I had done my homework. They expected me to be responsible and for the most part, I was. And when I wasn't, the fuss was minimal. I remember one time coming home way after midnight. My father met me at the door. He didn't scold me; he just looked me straight in the eye and asked, "Is this necessary?" My answer was a simple no. I never wanted to upset him. My mother collected my report cards because she was proud of them, but she never praised them, never said anything. It was just expected.

How was your relationship with those older sisters?

MC: They were fabulous and so good to me from the time I was little. They were closer to each other than to me because of the age difference. I was lucky. My family was warm and affectionate and funny. I think humor is a very Jewish thing. I didn't get it so much from my mother although she was my father's best audience. He always made her laugh. He saw humor in life where no one else looked. One day we were all getting dressed to go somewhere and all four of his daughters came into the kitchen where he was reading the paper. My mother wasn't ready yet. He looked up at us and said, "Girls, you look good, but not one of you can hold a candle to your mother." It could have left all of us scarred for life, but from him, it was just charming. The remark became a legend in the family. One of my sisters would say, "Listen, you look okay today, but you could never hold a candle to mom." And it was always funny. My husband had a great sense of humor. My children love to laugh but mostly at me.

When you got married, did you have your parents' marriage as an ideal in your head?

MC: Not consciously, but growing up in a house like that gives you a road map for a good marriage. There's a certain kind of give and take, generosity and consideration. I remember one Saturday I was working in the store with my dad and as we were leaving, he said he was tired and didn't want to go out that evening. He was going, he said, because my mother really needed to get out and be with friends. So we went home and while she was getting dressed, my mother and I talked. She said she didn't really want to go out but my dad worked hard and he needed to have some fun. I didn't say anything to either of them, but to me it was an example of the way they operated together. As the last daughter at home I was a witness to their relationship and I was old enough to understand it. Growing up with that relationship was very important in my life. I'm sure my parents had arguments, but I only remember them being very supportive of each other.

Did you have that in your marriage?

MC: Yes, but the marriage was not a carbon copy. My husband Don was a very different person. A friend recently said Don was a presence, and it was partly because he was a big man physically. He was very different from my father so our relationship was different from my parents'. My father was soft-spoken and gentle. Don had a booming voice and he was as impatient as my father was patient. But he was affectionate and steadfast and the marriage was important to him. He was my best friend. I hope he thought I was his. When there is a good marriage and the spouse dies, the loss is devastating. It shakes the foundation of your life. All three of my sisters were widowed. Two were in their early forties when their husbands died. I was in my early fifties. None of us ever married again. One of them had an opportunity to remarry, but didn't. She was left without much in the way of financial means and she had two sons, 9 and 10. Raising them, giving them everything they needed became the total focus of her life. She worked very hard and set an example of what had to be done to be successful in life--lessons that both of her sons learned well.

How do you define success?

MC: I can't tell you what that means exactly. There are variations on success, but if people are real and substantial, they are successful to me. The other thing is that no matter what you accomplish, if you aren't a caring human being, then what difference does anything make. Trite. But that's the way it is.

When you look back at your life do you have memories associated with certain times or decades?

MC: Tons of memories. Before Don got sick, they were mostly good memories…as a child, a young adult as a wife and mother. I think I was basically lazy, but I worked hard all my adult life. It wasn't easy, but it was good. I raised the kids and was involved in the community. There were wonderful milestones all along the way, but the darkest memory, the one that changed the direction of my life dominates all the others.

Can you tell us about that?

Don got sick when he was 52. He was playing tennis every day, was very athletic, and in much better shape than I. We'd just come back from Europe and he was having dizzy spells that doctors thought were related to an inner ear problem. Then he had a brain stem stroke. He was completely paralyzed except his cognitive brain function was unimpaired as far as the doctors could tell. So he was trapped in his body, locked in. Therapists taught him to communicate by blinking his eyes. We had a system in which I would spell out a few letters, he would blink to signal the right letter, and I would usually guess the rest. His illness marked the end of the happiest part of my life, and certainly it was horrible for him. If his thinking brain had been damaged, it would have been different. It might have been easier for him, but he was aware of everything. Doctors advised me to put him in a nursing home; however, I just couldn't. So we brought him home and I hired people to help because there was no way I could handle everything by myself. It was horrible.

Did he want to live?

MC: Yes, interestingly enough. At first he was very close to death. Doctors performed a tracheotomy and then a couple of weeks later, his doctor told me further drastic measures had to be taken to save his life. The doctor knew at that point Don wouldn't ever be able to move or speak. He needed my permission. I hesitated, not knowing whether Don would even want the life the doctor wanted to save. The doctor, whom I later learned was very religious, told me that if I didn't allow surgery to insert a feeding tube, he would leave the case. The threat was overwhelming. I don't think I had to the courage to pull the plug, but the doctor shouldn't have forced the decision. I learned later that other doctors were critical of him. Don was in the hospital for months for rehab. When he was stabilized and we had learned how to communicate I brought him home, bought a special bed and turned our bedroom into a hospital room. He lived two years and three months. It was awful for him, for me, and awful for the kids as well. I don't think Don ever lost hope about recovering because that was his personality.

How did Don finally die?

MC: He had another stroke or a heart attack. They didn't do an autopsy but it was one or the other. He'd been very restless and his breathing was labored. Several times previously we'd rushed him to the hospital, but that night he went to sleep and didn't wake up.

How did he spend his days if his brain was functioning?

MC: There was a program provided by the Library of Congress. You could borrow books on tape and they provided the equipment. We sent the tapes back and they would send new ones. We played them for him every day. How much he was able to take in, I don't know.

How old were you when this happened?

MC: I was 54. About a year after his stroke, I realized I was deteriorating. I was still teaching piano a bit, but some mornings I wasn't getting dressed. I was a mess. I heard the Community Relations Committee job was open and I'd been very active with the organization previously, so I called and asked if it was available. The director of the Jewish Federation said if I wanted the job it was mine. He didn't interview me. He just gave me the job. It was the fall of 1986. I started the job in March '87. I went to work with a great deal of guilt because I was leaving Don with strangers. But the work actually saved me. It was hard on him for me to be gone, but for a few hours a day, the work was engaging. I don't know what gave me the impetus to make that phone call; I just knew I was in trouble. That phone call saved me. The job gave me the opportunity to work on a multitude of issues that were interesting--Israel, anti-Semitism, inter-religious dialogues and dialogues with members of the African American and Hispanic communities and legislative issues. I also began to write a monthly column for the Jewish Journal. It was a new career, the end of one part of my life and beginning of the next.

How did you begin teaching about the Holocaust?

MC: In 1975 long before Don got sick, I got a call from the Community Relations Council. The director said they had been asked to provide a short educational Holocaust program for public high schools. I'd done a lot of reading about the subject. I was interested because of my family history, so I agreed to work as a volunteer. That first year we went to the local high schools with a 20-minute slide presentation followed by a discussion period. It was amateurish, but it was the best we had at that time. It was an experience I will never forget. It became very apparent that the subject engaged the students. They were discussing issues they'd never encountered. We continued to refine the script and add to the slide presentation. Don, who had a darkroom in the house, provided all the images and we constantly rewrote the program, adding details. At the beginning there were three of us making presentations and we were in the schools 2 or 3 times almost every week. Later there would be many more volunteers involved in the project including Holocaust survivors. We presented teachers' workshops all over the city and beyond.

Please tell us more about your intense interest in teaching about the Holocaust?

MC: I was still teaching piano, keeping house, and preparing meals, but I began to study the history of the Holocaust very seriously. My children used to tease me and call me Holocaust Hannah, because that's all I was reading. When Don had the stroke, I dropped all my volunteer work and didn't become involved in Holocaust education again until I took the job at the Jewish Federation. The Holocaust project was administered by the Community Relations Council (CRC). We were still sending volunteers into the schools. As the CRC director, I supervised the program but didn't teach. In the late 1980s, a number of Holocaust survivors in the community approached the Jewish Federation about establishing a memorial. We put an exhibit together in a large room in the old Federation building and enclosed a courtyard in which there were black granite panels that listed the names of the family members survivors had lost. There was a huge dedication ceremony with many people from the community attending including clergy and city officials. That exhibit did not attract many classes or visitors and we continued sending our volunteers out to the schools. But it was a major step because the education project was now linked formally to a site, a memorial. In 2000 when the Harry and Jeanette Weinberg Campus opened, the memorial was moved to the new location and an entirely new exhibit was created. In 1999, I had spoken to Mark Freedman, the Federation director, about retiring from the CRC. He asked if I could give him a year's notice, which I agreed to. As the year-end approached, however, I realized I still had enormous energy and there was no way I could retire. They were preparing to open the new Jewish Campus and I asked Mark whether I could work part time as the Holocaust Memorial director. He agreed and that was the beginning of another career. We were still sending volunteers into the schools with our program, but we knew the project could be more effective if teachers were to bring their classes into the memorial. The new exhibit was very meaningful, but it was designed more as a memorial than as a good teaching tool. We applied for a grant to re-do the exhibit. The goals, as I saw them at the time, were not only to teach the facts about what happened during the Nazi era, but also to help students seek out the story behind the facts. How and why did so many people, people not unlike the students themselves, become committed to a leader and a fanatic racist ideology that led to one of the greatest catastrophes in history? For me, the goal in teaching the Holocaust to American students is to make it relevant to their own lives, to help them understand that the choices they make, the leaders they follow, will shape their lives and the lives of others. It should help them define the roles they want to play as citizens and most importantly to help them think critically about their own attitudes towards people who are in some way different from them. Could we accomplish all of that that in the short time that students spend at the museum? No, but we thought we could start the process. Redoing the exhibit took two years. I worked with Marge Gregerman to gather the images and write the panels. When it was completed, we held a series of open houses to introduce educators to our efforts and it wasn't long before school buses were bringing classes in. The project blossomed. We did teacher training and provided programs for the community including the annual Yom HaShoah (a day to remember the Holocaust) commemoration. We provided speakers and materials for military bases and created an additional exhibit about anti-Semitism in the United States during the 1930s and 40s. With the help of a small group of public school teachers, we produced a book of local survivors' stories. Over time, my part time job had become full time and it was all consuming, but one day, I walked into my office and realized I wasn't totally engaged anymore. It was the signal. In 2010, I decided that I had had enough. I retired.

Did you panic again about retiring?

MC: I did. I knew the time had come for me to walk away, but it was very hard. I saw things change and I didn't like it. In a sense it was my baby, and I had very strong ideas about the direction the museum should take. It took me a while to stand back and see that change was necessary, but it wasn't easy.

What do you think of the idea of presenting Jews as victims?

MC: Through the centuries Jews have been victims and in some places continue to be even today, but there is much more to the story. The history of Jews is amazing. It's filled with triumphs as well as tragedy. I don't think all Jews are virtuous or clever, but their accomplishments in science, the arts, business and other fields are remarkable. I'm teaching a course about Israel in the fall and I marvel at the strength and ingenuity of the Jews who founded that country. So, yes, Jews have been victimized, but they haven't been defeated by it.

When you started working with the Holocaust programs did you develop a stronger Jewish identity?

MC: I always had a strong Jewish identity, although I'm not religious. I think it has a lot to do with how I felt about my parents and their values. My work may have increased the identity, but it was always there. Going to school where I was the only Jewish child probably increased that identification as well.

Did the feminist movement affect you?

MC: How could it! I was raised in a family of four girls. The one to feel sorry for was my father. It was impossible to feel downtrodden. And from my mother, I certainly didn't get the idea that a woman couldn't fulfill her dreams or ambition. But it is true that if I hadn't been a woman I probably would have had greater financial expectations and made more money. Was I aggressive enough pushing for my salary? No. For a while, I was working full time for part time pay. No man would have done that. So that was stupid, and it was certainly part of my identity as a woman. But in terms of growing up with the feeling that women couldn't do what they wanted, I never had that.

Did Don value that?

MC: Don wanted a partner and made that clear. He was a forceful personality, but he didn't expect me to be a submissive. On our second date he told me he thought we should get married. I thought he was crazy. But I learned that that's the way he was. He made quick decisions, but the decisions were not made without consulting me.

Did you envision your life when you were younger? Did you have a preconceived notion of your future?

MC: No. Absolutely not. If I had, I think I would have been more thoughtful. I'll tell you something interesting. I'd forgotten about this, but when I was 14 or so, my mother came to me and said, "You know, you are going to need a career." At the time I wondered if she thought I'd never get married. She said, "You're not going to be happy without a career." I didn't pay any attention then. I understand now what she was saying, and I appreciate it. In many ways she was a modern woman.

When you look at your life, other than Don's stroke, do you see major changes or choices?

MC: Outside factors have a lot to do with decisions. If I hadn't married young, if I'd had fewer children, my life would have been different. Raising children consumed a large portion of my life, and I don't regret it. But it's impossible to exaggerate the impact of Don's illness and death. It changed the entire trajectory of my life in terms of work and lifestyle. Some of the changes were positive, but some of the choices I made came about as a result of unhappy circumstances.

How important are your friendships with other women?

MC: They are vitally important along with my relationships with my children and grandchildren. After Don's death, many of my old friendships and couple friendships fell by the wayside. I was the first widow--a kind of "Other." It was lonely. Finding women who shared some of the things I do and cared about each other was essential. I was lucky to find them.

What brings you bliss?

MC: I am happiest when my family is together. No question. I also love to be with friends. That's very important to me, but bliss is watching my family interact and laugh. My older son called the other day and he was talking about how close he is to his brother. I teased him and asked when was the last time he talked to his brother? He said, "I don't have to talk to him to feel close." I think that is true. There is a bond among the children that is beautiful to see.

Are all your children funny?

MC: Yes, and so are the grandchildren.

Most people, including me, have memory issues as they age? Do you?

MC: Some memory loss started in my 50s. Yet, the other day I was talking with my son about President Roosevelt and I was able to name part of his cabinet. My son was floored. So was I. But on a day-to-day basis, retrieval of information is much slower than it used to be and sometimes, it doesn't happen at all...very frustrating.

Does memory affect playing the piano?

MC: I don't play very much anymore because of my arthritic hands. But if I pick up a piece I haven't touched in 40 years, I can learn it; if I pick up a new piece, I can't. There's some sort of tactile memory. My fingers remember...like riding a bike I suppose.

Do you remember learning to ride? Did you have training wheels?

MC: I had a red bike and no training wheels. They didn't use them in my day. I had three sisters and I'd get on the bike and a sister would run along beside me until I was okay.

Are you a fearless person in general?

MC: I don't think I'm fearless, but there's not much I'm afraid of anymore. I am afraid of being helpless but not many other things. It's one of the few blessings of old age. You see things differently and that creates less fear. I worry about the state of the world and if something terrible happened to my children I'd be undone, but in a general sense, I'm not afraid.

Just of being helpless?

MC: I am terrified of that.

Physically?

MC: That's part of it, but mentally too.

Is that a fear you had before Don had the stroke?

MC: Yes, because previously I watched my father wither away. That's what I'm afraid of. The rest of it I'll figure out.

Don't you reach an age and figure, "I've survived so far. What can happen?"

MC: That's exactly it. So far I've made it… somehow. My son moved out of town recently and that was a major change. It was not that I was dependent on him. I'm pretty independent, but not having any of my children close by was unsettling. I was uncomfortable for a while but I adjusted, came to terms with the problem and realized I could handle it. I have friends I can call. I have a life to live.

Have you thought about what you'll do when you enter a stage when you can't be independent?

MC: I don't have a plan but I do think about it. The one thing I will not do is live with my children. If I do need someone to take care of me, I don't want it to be my children.

You want to stay at home?

MC: Yes, as long as I can. It's important for me to be in charge of my own life in my own place. If I could live independently until I die, that would be the greatest gift of all. I'd like to end with a funny family story. A while ago, I found a big snake in my garage. I called my son to deal with it. When he saw the snake, he picked it up very gently and carefully. He tenderly wrapped it in a towel and took it way. When I asked him if he would treat me with such tender care, he laughed and said, "Don't count on it!"

Lifetime San Antonio resident, Anita Valencia developed as an artist in her middle age and is now one of San Antonio's major public artists. Her early work included paintings and prints. However, in recent years her art has become much more daring. Her entirely recycled materials silently shout about the volume of junk we throw away and thus serve an important ecological purpose; simultaneously, her recycle creations are magical and beautiful in the way they transform garbage into art.

ANITA VALENCIA

Let's start with all the lovely things we see here in this room. Did you make that wall hanging?

AV: Yes, that's one of the first things I made when I returned from Japan. It's origami.

I think I've seen your work around San Antonio! Do you have pieces hanging at the Blood and Tissue Center and at the Hyatt downtown?

AV: Yes, both.

They've always been some of my favorite pieces. And now I am meeting you! My favorite thing about donating platelets is being able to see your piece every time I go. This piece over here is fantastic.

AV: Those pieces are made from recycled shopping bags. Do you remember when HEB had paper grocery bags?

Did you say you learned origami in Japan?

AV: I didn't really learn there. What I did was observe Japanese people folding and then came home and got a bunch of books and taught myself. The focus of that trip was papermaking, but it turned out that wasn't what interested me. It was origami.

Was that the first time you made anything? Your first art endeavor?

AV: As far as recycled art, yes. I had been printmaking for years, and you know you have to make tons of proofs and I couldn't stand the waste. One day I was reading an article titled something like "If you have these things in your kitchen you too can make paper." I'll never forget it. And I did. I had everything I needed and started to make paper with my own discarded proofs. A few years later I learned about this international papermaking conference in Japan; a friend and I applied and they accepted us. We were surprised but happy. I submitted a piece of paper I had made from tamale husks. It was so fragile and so beautiful. I think it was unusual and that's why they accepted me. Many of the Asian countries make beautiful paper. We even saw papyrus being made; that was very interesting because they actually pound the strips together.

When did you start making paper?

AV: About 1979 and we went to the conference in Japan in 1983. When I returned I started making origami with all my wasted paper. I don't do much with paper anymore. I use soda cans and other materials but I cut and fold whatever it is.

What kind of art did you make before you made paper?

AV: I used to paint. Large paintings in both oil and acrylic.

It sounds like you've been an artist all your life and just kept switching mediums.

AV: Yes, I like to say I was evolving. One thing led to another. One idea leads to another idea.

Did that happen because you got bored with one thing and were looking for something new?

AV: No, I don't think so. All of a sudden I'll have an idea and think maybe I can expand this piece I am working on another way or do something differently. For instance, recently piles of CDs are being thrown in the trash, so I've started working with CDs and making collages and sculptures with them. That's easier on my hands since I have carpel tunnel. Obviously, I hope my art brings attention to how much we all waste.

Couldn't you hire people to construct your design, to embody your ideas?

AV: That's what happened with the bench the River Authority commissioned on the river. Other people actually built it. They had a fabricator do it. It's along the southern reach mission trail by the Lone Star Brewery area.

So you painted early in your career and that was more marketable.

AV: Oh yes. Sometimes I sold paintings right off my easels.

Isn't most of your newer work public art rather than small pieces made for individual collectors?

AV: Yes, I like doing public art. That way more people get to see it and enjoy it. When you see a huge construction made of bottle caps, you understand how every single piece of garbage we throw in the street is one of millions and matters! One of my favorite pieces was on exhibit at the airport a few years ago. I made a quilt out of old cigarette wrappers. It was huge. It was one of the first exhibits of public art at the airport. It was fun collecting the wrappers. I even brought some from Paris!

You have a lot of public art installed here in San Antonio. Anywhere else?

AV: Only in Montreal at the Omni Hotel. It's a piece made out of beer cans. I had all my friends drink different kinds of beer and save their empty cans for me. The installation was of 400 "BEERflies"! Here's a bizarre story: on the way to meet with the committee to discuss my proposal when the Grand Hyatt was being built here, I twisted my knee as I got out of the car. I had to be carried into the meeting! I could tell by the looks on the faces of the very proper women from Dallas who were the designers that they thought I was a helpless old woman. One woman even said, "Are you sure she can do anything?" Just like that. I thought well, there goes my commission. But, they accepted it.

It's great that so many hotels are incorporating art exhibits into their design.

AV: It is. It's another way to expose people to art and another market for artists.

San Antonio seems to have gotten more sophisticated lately regarding art. Is it a supportive community?

AV: It is, but we need more collectors. There aren't many.

Where do you sell most of your art?

AV: I don't have a gallery anymore since the one I used closed. I don't like selling on my own. One of the reasons I like doing public art is because they tell me right off how much money they have and then I make designs to fit that amount. I don't have to haggle. I've been so lucky to be approached, since psychologically I really can't go out and market or promote myself. I just can't do that.

Have you ever worked with other artists?

AV: Not really. I am pretty solitary when I'm in my studio. I don't even turn on the radio. I just really get into what I'm doing and the time flies by. But I've had a lot of help with my installations. I could not have installed "CANdelier" and "Aguaceros" without help from Abigale and Stan Kline and my husband. Abigale worked out very complicated details for both installations, and all three helped install them. And for my installation at the Southwest School of Art, "The Sun she rise, the sun she set and you ain't seen all of Texas yet," Abigale and Roland Pena pinned hundreds of butterflies to the wall and Stan installed the "Tornado."

Have you always supported yourself with your art?

AV: Well, not really. My husband supported me and was happy to do it. He was very sweet about it. He never complained when I made a piece that took up half the house! And my mother helped with my children and she paid for my art classes at the San Antonio Art Institute. She told me early on not to stay home with my kids and she volunteered to take care of my kids while I went to art classes. She told me I had to stay interesting.

Interesting or interested?

AV: Interesting. Be interesting. She was a Mexican mother, mind you! She was very much ahead of her time. She had two children and said, "A boy and a girl; that's all we need." When I was young, I was very religious, and I said, "Oh Mom, you're going to go to hell," and she said, "I'm not going to let men tell me what to do."

I love that she enabled you to pursue your art. She didn't just say you should, she volunteered to help with your family and paid for the class.

AV: All my children have always been very supportive but it was my youngest daughter, Esther, who enabled my education. When I was young I went to San Antonio College for two years; UTSA didn't exist in those years, so I couldn't earn a Bachelor's degree. Years later Esther registered at UTSA and came home one day and informed me she had gotten me an advisor and brought home the materials I needed to apply to go back to school. By that time one son was in grade school and the other in high school. At first we had three daughters and that was it. Seven years later we had a surprise and seven years after that we had another surprise. Those were our two sons. Anyway, my daughter Esther got me registered at UTSA and I was petrified. She took me to the class and when I came out she was waiting for me and said "Now was it all that hard?" She talked to me the way I had talked to her when she was beginning kindergarten!

How old were you then?

AV: About 48. I hadn't been to school since before I was married. I took English and philosophy and got my humanities degree, thanks to my daughter. I wanted to learn why I made art, not how to make it.

Had you been making art before you went to UTSA?

AV: Mostly just helping with school projects with the kids and things like that. Nothing serious until I went to the Art Institute that was part of the McNay Art Museum.

And when was that?

AV: In the late 70s. I was in my early forties. I made a lot of good friends there. They had printmaking, ceramics and painting. I took painting from Reggie Rowe. I also took printmaking from Kent Rush.

Did you ever consider teaching art?

AV: No. I don't mind giving demos or working with an occasional student, but I am not cut out to be a teacher.

Did any of your five children inherit an interest in art from you?

AV: One of my sons is an executive pastry chef in Manhattan. He makes beautiful things. My oldest daughter is a computer scientist. My second daughter, who passed away, was a lawyer in intellectual property. My third daughter earned a PhD in chemistry and then went into entomology and worked with the USDA, but now she stays home and works in her garden. My other son lives in New Mexico where he went to New Mexico University. He got interested in racecars and builds them. But then he started to breed sea horses and growing coral. He's gotten so good that he has a worldwide reputation.

Let's talk more about your recycle art–converting trash into beauty.

AV: I've worked with candy wrappers, coat hangers, bottle tops, pull back tabs, panty hose, you name it.

When you conceptualize something, do you draw it or do you build it in your brain?

AV: I can't draw what I'm thinking. That's the hard part of commissions. I have to submit so many drawings, and the concept cannot really change or grow. For the large pieces I have to make a pattern so the installers know where the pieces go. I have to mark the pieces and designate them on the pattern.

Let's go upstairs and take a look at your studio.

AV: This is the house I lived in with my parents. When I got married, my husband and I lived nearby and then moved in here later. At the top of the stairs on the left is the room I had as a girl. The room on the right was my brother's. Now, it's where I store my completed pieces.

I love this screen with the family photos.

AV: I made that for my mom when she got Alzheimer's. She loved to sit and look at it and see all the various members of her family. So, over here is my studio. This was a porch when I was growing up.

This piece is fabulous! What colors!

AV: It just came back from the "50 at 50" show at the Southwest School of Art. It's made of candy wrappers. I had so much fun making it, even though it took forever. Over there, see those? That's one of the first things I did when I came back from Japan. They are pagodas.

What are you working on now?

Nothing. I'm going through a lull.

What inspires you?

AV: Nothing in particular. Somehow something comes up in my mind and I know it's what I need to do. Over here is a series of eight or nine because they just kept going. I couldn't stop. These are old paintings that I had but I didn't like them anymore so I covered them. More recycling. Let me show you something. Here at the top of these stairs with my room on the left and my brother's on the right, this is where the original house ended. Then my mother, going back to being a Mexican mother, didn't want her son to leave, so she built an apartment for him and added this part of the house. Now my daughter uses it when she comes to visit. Over there is a portrait I made of my mother when she had Alzheimer and would sit in the garden with me.

The face and hands look different than the rest of the piece.

AV: Yes, I painted those. The rest is pieces of paper. Over there are more CD sculptures. Look how the sunlight reflects off of them. Over here is a bottle cap collage. I like to work with the colors and patterns. I usually start in the corner and work up and sometimes I end up having to repaint some of the caps to fit with the scheme. One of the things I sold recently was a giant paper butterfly I made from recycling some of my old prints that I no longer liked. First I made them into paper and then the butterfly.

Tell us about growing up in San Antonio and living across from Woodlawn Lake.

AV: Actually I grew up on the West side and didn't move here until I was about 18. My parents saw this house one day when they were driving by, fell in love with it, and bought it. My father was a grocer; our home and store were one big building. In those days all the neighborhoods had their own little grocery store. I was lucky to live in that neighborhood. We had the Edelmans, the Jones, the Gonzales-- all mixed up. I didn't know if we were rich or poor and there were all kinds of churches. We all played together. My father instilled the love of reading in me. He was the youngest son and was sent to work for a rich uncle while his two older brothers attended pharmacy school. The deal was that when they obtained their degrees, it would be my father's turn. Of course, they got married, started families, and my dad never got his education. But he loved to read and was especially fond of poetry. I still have his poetry book, "Campoamor Poesias." After a very hard day of work in his grocery store, he would relax reading and often reciting his favorite poem by Sor Juana de la Cruz, "Hombres Necios."

Tell me about the piano here. It's beautiful.

AV: My dad thought I was a child prodigy and this poor lady would come to our house to teach me piano for only ten cents a class or something like that. I hated piano! I took lessons for years and years. Then my dad sacrificed and bought me this piano. A baby grand for the child prodigy, you know! It wasn't until I got to college that a teacher told me I was tone deaf! On and off my kids played and took lessons. But you know, I can't get rid of it. It reminds me of my dad's sacrifice.

When you were a little girl were you interested in art?

AV: Yes, in school the nuns would always say let Anita do the drawings because she's the artist. Everyone always assumed I would do it.

One of your daughters died when she was young and a few months ago your husband died. How has loss affected you?

AV: My mother was the hardest. She had Alzheimer's for years. It was very hard. She didn't want to be alone. She had lived through the Mexican revolution and at the end of her life she thought the revolution was still going on and that violent men would break into the house. Her family had lived in the middle of Mexico City during the revolution and she said a rebel company would come in and take over a house and the maids would hide the children and women under the floor planks so the armed men couldn't take them. Her much older sister married an American traveling salesman from Macon, Georgia and he brought my mother's sister and my mother to the US where she traveled all over the US with them. Then the couple decided my mother needed to go to school and that they needed to settle down. They liked San Antonio because it had a lot of Spanish-speaking people so they rented a house and my mother and grandmother lived there with them.

In addition to making art, are you active in the art community?

AV: Oh yes. For example, I'm on the board of the Tres Centurias for public sculpture in the new Hemisphere Park. I'm hoping to get some local sculptors commissioned. There's a push to get "big" names brought in but I really hope most of the commissions go to our local artists.

What do you do in your down time?

AV: I love to read and I'm currently reading a book about the Wright Brothers. It's fascinating how they studied birds and applied that knowledge to their designs. It's also interesting to read about all the naysayers, their contemporaries who insisted human beings could never fly.

Have you had naysayers about your art, which certainly isn't traditional or conventional?

AV: No, I've been very lucky. Early on I applied to every juried show and then I got that first big commission at the Blood Bank. Now the work comes to me.

Is there something you want to do? Did you have goals when you were young?

AV: No, not really. I always seem to be happy in the state I'm in. If I want to do something, it just sort of happens. One thing leads to another.

Do you work on your art every day?

AV: Yes. I may not work but I go into the studio every day and clean and move things around and think.

Brought up in East Texas oil fields by her grandparents after her parents divorced, Lea Glisson had a challenging early life. After attending junior college on a band scholarship, she took her life into her own hands, and, step by step, made herself into a highly successful civil servant with the U.S. Military. The high-ranking officers she worked for served as role models for her. Using her inner strength and "streak of oil field toughness," she successfully survived a devastating divorce, which followed thirty-eight years of marriage. Since she retired, she has published two memoirs of her childhood of poverty and Pentecostal religion, and she continues to write stories and articles.

LEATHA DAILEY GLISSON

Lea, I know you've written <u>Some Glad Morning</u>, a memoir about your childhood, but I still want to hear you talk about it for us.

L: I was born in Longview, Texas, which is perhaps eighty miles from the Louisiana border. My father worked in oil fields. When I was one-and a half and my brother Reuben was three, my parents divorced.

Divorce was unusual in those days and particularly in a rural area, wasn't it? Why did they divorce?

L: They divorced because my father was a gorgeous man who women loved and he loved them! My mother was actually my father's second wife. At around 18 or 19 my father married a girl who was the love of his life, I think. She slipped out of the window of her parents' house and they ran off together. The next day her father was going to chase them with a shotgun, but her sister told him that they probably had already slept together! My father's first wife got pregnant soon after they married and his young wife and the newborn died in childbirth. I don't think my father ever loved that deeply again. Nobody ever talked about it.

So, back to your parents' marriage and divorce.

L: At the time of the divorce my mother was still very young, maybe 18 or 19, with little money or education. We never talked about why Reuben and I were living with my father's parents whom we called Mama and HaHa. My father lived close by, but we lived with his parents. My father visited us frequently, but I didn't see my mother that often because my stepfather worked in the oil field in New Mexico, Oklahoma, and the Texas panhandle. Mama, my grandmother, didn't like my mother although she was too religious to be overtly critical of her. I know that she did not like that my mother was a carhop and served beer. I, secretly, liked that about my mother. She wore a pretty uniform and looked very good in it. In truth, my mother was one of the nicest people in the world. One good thing is that after my parents divorced and years later married other people and had more children, they remained perfectly friendly and cordial with each other.

Tell us about life with Mama and HaHa.

L: By far the most important person in my early life was Mama. She was 65 when she began taking care of Reuben and me. My father provided financial support for us, but the Depression was a difficult time. My grandfather kept a garden and we had a cow and chickens to supplement the income. Mama made many of my dresses out of feed sacks. She always seemed to me to be a sad, old woman. She was very strict, spent any spare time reading the Bible and seemed more interested in life after death than in everyday life. She was a superstitious and Pentecostal woman. Mama's Pentecostal relatives would visit from deep East Texas; they would stay about a week and it would be like an old tent revival. They would read the Bible and get down on their knees and start speaking in tongues, which scared me to death. The sound of those words terrified me and I ran outside. Reuben and I were not allowed to have cards or go to the movies. Mama would have died and "be to bury" if we had done sinful things like that. "Be to bury" is an east Texas phrase, which means would have died. Years later when I worked for the Air Force, my military co-workers from other parts of the country would make fun of my expressions, and I had to translate for them half of what I said! My seventh grade teacher was the first person that told me I was pretty. She said I had the most beautiful blue eyes she had ever seen. Well, I thought I had died and gone to heaven. To Mama if you looked too good, you were likely to be prideful and that was a sin. You would be studying yourself instead of the Bible and praying. Mama told me exactly what to do and when to do it, even when to breathe in and out, it seemed.

Was HaHa also a Pentecostal?

L: I don't know that my grandfather had any religion. I remember him as a big, very quiet man.

Tell us about a typical day in your childhood—maybe age ten.

L: Let's see. At ten I was in the seventh grade.

What? How can that be?

L: Because of Mama. Reuben started school before me, since he was older. When he came home to do his homework, Mama sat me down beside him and I did the same work. Mama had a teacher mentality. Learning was important to her. Reading the Bible was most important, of course, but she encouraged reading in general. When it was time for me to start school the next year, Mama wanted me to be in the second grade with Reuben. She went to the school and explained that to the superintendent. He said I could try second grade for six weeks and if I couldn't do the work I would go back to first grade. We lived in Longview in the oil field where my dad was working until I was about eight or nine when we moved to Panola County into a house on the bluff overlooking the Sabine River. A black family lived in the only other house we could see from ours. They were a couple, Clarence and Essie, who had two daughters in their late teens and a son in his early twenties.

Were you allowed to visit this black family?

L: Oh no, we could barely look at the house! The funny thing was that Essie cooked for my other grandmother. I'd slip down to the forbidden house if Mama was taking a nap. They had an organ one of the daughters let me play. She would work the pedals and I'd play the keys! Essie made the best cornbread, but Mama would never allow me to eat in their house. I never lived in a painted house until 1950 when we moved to Tyler. The house was simple; my grandfather built the fireplace, the kitchen had a wood-burning stove, and there was a junk room. That junk room is the reason I don't have any junk in my house. I remember with pleasure the whole process of Mama making biscuits.

Do you still make them the same way?

L: Oh no! I don't cook—not since I found out there were grocery stores where you could buy things.

You really don't cook at all?

L: Well, I'm a really good cook, but I keep that fact hidden.

Tell us a bit more about your grandfather.

L: He was a carpenter and brick mason and when he retired, he got what they called an old age pension. Today it probably wouldn't buy a Starbucks' latte!

After high school, what did you do?

L: My brother and I both got band scholarships to Tyler Junior College, so the family moved to Tyler.

Were you always a good student?

L: I loved school and never, ever missed a day. I would have gone to school if I was dying! Books were my friends all my life.

Growing up smart and eager to learn, were you eager to leave east Texas?

L: Yes, and I did the day I graduated from Tyler Junior College. I didn't move out of Texas because my work kept me in the state, but I never went back to live in east Texas except when I was doing research for my memoir about growing up there. Once I was acclimated to life in the city, the deep conservatism and lack of inclusiveness in some parts of east Texas became troublesome for me. Yet I admire the work ethic they instilled in me. They received no help from the government until they got their old age pensions and even then my grandfather worked. I'm 81 and still some days I feel guilty if I don't accomplish something!

When and how did you meet your ex-husband?

L: I met him on a blind date during my sophomore year in college. He was in the Air Force, and a mutual friend set us up. Believe it or not, he would hitchhike something like 300 or 400 miles from his Air Force base in Wichita Falls to Tyler so we could have dates. We probably had eight dates before we eloped to Texarkana, Arkansas. Food was a very important thing in my ex-husband's life. He grew up in a family in south Georgia where they sat down "feet under the table" three times a day and ate full meals. He expected that when he married me. And I was a person who didn't want to do anything but read books! I learned how to cook and we sat down three times a day; but the minute he left my house after 38 years of marriage when he was 55, I said, "I'm not going to cook another meal."

After 38 years of marriage his departure must have been very hard for you.

L: We had a really good marriage for 38 years. I made the decision I would not throw that away and live my life in bitterness, so I took steps to start a new life as a single woman. He died earlier this year. I miss him every day.

Tell us about your adjustment to the end of the marriage.

L: It was awful at first. We grew up together, and came out of the country together, we educated ourselves together, and we read etiquette books and learned how to give parties. We constructed new selves together. Sometimes I would sit here looking at the crumbles of our marriage and think I was not going to get out of bed. But I had our daughter and grandson and a streak of oil field toughness. I told myself that I had to choose whether to live or die and I chose to live. I didn't miss a day of work even though I had to drive by myself to the same place where we had driven together and worked together for years. For a while I thought that as long as his valuable tools remained in the garage he would come back. But one day he called and said he was coming by to pick up his tools. After that I knew it was really over, and I found it hard to return home after work. In order to heal, I decided I would do whatever I wanted. I would go to a movie after work to avoid going home. I went to every lecture or exhibit in the city. I took every kind of continuing education class. At one of these lectures I heard a psychiatrist say something that really resonated. He said that every time you relive a horrible situation in your mind, your body is reacting the way it did when the event occurred. You're damaging your liver, your lungs, and so on. I told myself that Bill was living a new life while I was killing myself. That was when I began to heal. It took me about three years.

Did you get any professional help?

L: Being an educated person I went to a therapist who told me something I would never have thought of, but which was undoubtedly true. He said that my husband leaving the marriage was a second abandonment for me. That not growing up with my parents was abandonment for me as a child, and that I needed to reintegrate my adult and child selves. Of course, I then bought all the self-help books I could find, because you know I love words and books.

Did anything else help?

L: Yes, indeed. Whatever else Mama did, she made me a praying person. I knew that I had to let go of what I perceived as the reasons Bill left our marriage. As long as I kept them in the front of my mind, I was hurting myself, so one night I lay in bed and said, "God, I am giving this anger to you. From now on, I am letting go of the people and circumstances that are causing physical and emotional turmoil in my life." It was like a salvation experience. This heaviness lifted and I began to heal.

Did your friends help you through this transition?

L: I had and still have many friends, but I went through it alone by choice. I need to be alone when I grieve or am sick. Everybody offered to help, but I didn't let them. I went to therapy, Bible study, and social events. My job required that I travel sometimes. To a degree my job itself helped me keep balanced.

When did you retire?

L: In 1993. When I got my master's degree at 49; I wanted to go on for a PhD but you can't retire from the government until you are 55, and I needed the retirement annuity. My civil service grade ensured a good income and I was told getting a PhD would just make me over-qualified for most jobs.

You've written two memoirs. When you're not writing books, what do you read?

L: I love murder mysteries, history, biography. I do a lot of research on my computer. I have an iPhone, iPad and Mac. I love watching sports, especially basketball. Before we divorced, my husband and I had season tickets three rows from the floor for the Spurs games. I play games and puzzles on my iPad. I think I'm the only person in the USA who doesn't know how to play solitaire. You know Mama would never let us have cards. One time my brother came home with a deck of cards; Mama took one look, grabbed the cards, and dropped them into the wood stove! When I watch TV, I turn on the mute and read during commercials. But sometimes I get so involved with my reading I miss the rest of the show.

What was the greatest example of cause and effect in your life?

L: Because I grew up with such limited control of my life, I got the best education I could get and the best job I could find in order to live the life I wanted to live.

What was the major fork in your journey?

L: Getting married at 17.

Do you think you shaped your life or your life shaped you?

L: I shaped it.

Are you a rule obeyer?

L: I never saw a rule I didn't challenge. If they make sense, I follow them. Things need to have some modicum of sense and logic.

Are you the same on the inside as on the outside?

L: I think I'm tougher on the outside than on the inside. If I hurt someone's feelings, I have to make it right.

Do you ever shock yourself?

L: Several times a day! I see a man and wonder what it would like to have him as my husband. Mama would think that was bad.

Besides words and books, what provides sustenance for you?

L: Ice cream.

What robs you emotionally?

L: Concern for the welfare of the people I love.

Do you worry?

L: I have to say the serenity prayer all day long.

Do you have a daily routine?

L: Absolutely. I get up, take my pills, make my coffee. I look for my newspaper and if it hasn't been delivered yet, I am not a happy woman. I sit down and drink coffee with my left hand and hold the paper with my right hand. I never eat at a table; I eat breakfast, lunch and dinner sitting in a chair holding a tray. Dinner is usually popcorn. This is going to knock your hat in the creek, but I love McDonalds soft serve ice cream because it's not too sweet and has exactly the right texture. I drive there every day; they know me and my car at the drive-through window. I don't even have to order. They know I want a plain sundae. I've watched "The Young and the Restless" and "Days of our Lives" for forty years! I record them on the DVR so I can skip the commercials. After that I chew two pieces of chewing gum, because I've heard that is good for your teeth. As you can tell, I tend to be a little OCD. I'm always straightening towels, the things in my cupboard all face the same way, my clothes are color-coordinated. Here's a funny example. For some reason, my husband had the bedroom closet door alarmed as well as the usual things. One night I decided that instead of hanging up my robe before going to sleep I would just lay it across the bed. But I couldn't sleep because my robe was not where it should be, so I got up, picked up the robe and opened the door to the closet—and set off this terrible loud alarm! I think my compulsive neatness grew out of that junk room.

Did you ever have a mentor?

L: All the high-ranking officers I worked for were mentors to me. The majority of my supervisors were colonel or general rank and physicians. I learned about relationships with people when I listened to how they talked to their officers. I learned how to interpret people and to describe them. I modeled myself after smart, successful men. The officers' wives would always refer to me as the general's secretary instead of by my name. We went to parties all the time and one of the wives introduced herself to me again and again. It was a putdown. One time I finally said, "I know who you are. You always introduce yourself to me." Generally in the workplace I like men better than women. When I was young, the women just wanted to talk about their kids and cakes. I always worked. I wasn't interested in that. Where I grew up, women made the men's plates and took the plates of food to them. When I married, I told Bill, "I am not your mother. I will not be making your plate."

What is your biggest accomplishment?

L: To go from growing up with a junk room to earning a Master of Liberal Studies degree from the University of Oklahoma to having a long, successful career. I am always learning, in or out of a classroom. At one time I thought we'd invest in real estate so I took the classes and got a real estate license. Because I love style and fashion, I took modeling lessons and did that for a while. Because I love history, I became a docent in a museum and one day the group suggested I become a tour guide. San Antonio has a professional association for tour guides, so I studied for months, took the test and was certified. At one point after I retired I had a job as the scheduling secretary for the San Antonio mayor. I got to do wonderful things through that job even though I worked harder for less money than I was paid previously. Years later Fiesta royalty asked me to be their scheduling secretary. That's when I met a prominent local woman who hired me to be her social secretary, and I worked for her for five years. I wrote my two books, learned about publishing a book, established my own business, self-published the books, got the copyrights, marketed them and did it all myself. The important things in my life are God, family and country. I'm a very patriotic person. I love the flag and the liberty and freedom it stands for. I love learning and new ideas. The liberal studies classes taught me to think outside the paradigm. I've always wanted to learn and tell stories. My life is a journey waiting to be told or written.

After her first six years living in a tenement in Spanish Harlem, Nereida Reyes moved to Fort Greene Projects in Brooklyn, which she thought was like heaven, because there was more than one window. After a teenage pregnancy, shotgun marriage, domestic abuse, flight to California, and other difficulties, she finally fulfilled her life dream of higher education and now at 80 is a beloved tutor at St. Philip's College helping young people with their struggles and English grammar. She loves to cook her Puerto Rican specialties and talks about praying over her pots—one of which is a family heirloom.

NEREIDA REYES

Let's start with those photos on your wall, particularly the large wedding photo.

NR: That is my mother and father. They had their wedding picture enlarged for their 50th wedding anniversary. My daughter, who is a student in the culinary arts at St Philip's College, framed all the photographs on the wall. For many years she had the photo of mom and dad, then when she moved out of her home in Houston, the photo came home to me. The top photo is my brother who passed away in 2003. My brother was taking photography at UTSA and he took the self-photo as a class project. The next photo was taken when I was a bridesmaid is my cousin's wedding. The next photo, the skyscraper, is the Williamsburg Bank building; at the time it was the tallest building in Brooklyn. During my childhood in Brooklyn we didn't have a man coming around the neighborhoods with a pony for the kids to ride as well as to take their photo. But there was a man who came to our neighborhood, got all the kids together, and took group pictures. That's one that includes me. The next photo is my father and a friend and a bicycle that has a large basket in the front.

Are they selling something on that bike?

NR: No, my grandfather owned a grocery store in Puerto Rico; he was also a bootlegger of moonshine. My dad would deliver groceries, as well as moonshine, I'm sure, to neighbors in the barrio.

So you are Puerto Rican.

NR: Yes, first generation born in the US. I grew up in the Fort Greene projects in Brooklyn. It was like Disneyland for my brother and me.

Really? In what way?

NR: Because we had moved out of the tenements in Spanish Harlem into Brooklyn in 1942, and the project buildings had windows! I finally had my own bedroom and my younger brothers shared a room. One of the windows in my bedroom faced my public school, P.S. 67, and the Walt Whitman Library. The other window faced St. Edwards Church and St. Edwards Street. I could sit on my windowsill, look out the window and count the cars as they passed by. But the best part was watching the winter snow flurries sparkle under the lampposts. It was like magic.

You didn't have windows in Spanish Harlem?

NR: Oh no! Tenements have one window. They are long like a train boxcar and the living room, which always faced the street, had the one window. The other rooms did not have windows. Yet I seem to remember that the small kitchen had a small window facing an alley.

How many years did you live in the tenements?

NR: Six years. From birth to age six. Then we moved to the projects where we had City Park to the north and Fort Greene Park to the south and we had free rein of the neighborhood.

So the neighborhood was safe?

NR: It was so safe! We could stay out sometimes until 11 o'clock at night playing in the schoolyard. Handball, ringalevio, kick the can.

Ringalevio?

NR: Yes! You don't know it? Ringalevio 1, 2, 3? Everybody scattered at three and whoever was "it" had to look for you. Like hide and seek.

You went to school in Brooklyn?

NR: Yes, public school. There were six kids in our family and I was the only girl and the oldest child. I would enjoy playing school with my brothers because I was always the teacher.

Were you spoiled because you were the only girl?

NR: No, I don't think so. I was the mother to the three youngest brothers. I fed them, washed diapers, took them to the doctor. I mean, my mom cooked but she was overwhelmed. My older brothers worked for Zeppelin Grocery Store on the corner. The boys delivered the groceries to the homes in brown paper sacks and cardboard boxes. I was always on the lookout for my brothers because bullying was going on even back then. It's a wonderful feeling when I visit my brothers, who live out of state, talking about memories and sharing how much we love each other.

What about your teenage years?

NR: My teen years were difficult because my mom placed a lot of responsibility on me, especially caring for my siblings. Also, my mother had told me to avoid being friends with young black boys, so out of rebellion I sought them out. I began a relationship with the boy who became my husband out of rebellion but later stayed in it out of fear of him. In my senior year I got pregnant. I did not know how babies were made. I had no clue.

Your parents never said don't do this or that?

NR: All they said was "Keep your legs crossed!" But they never said why! After having all those boys, my mom wasn't going to take care of another baby, so we had what was called in those days a shotgun wedding. We got married, my mother wouldn't come to the church, and he went into the military.

How old were the two of you?

NR: He was 17 and I was 16. He dropped out of school too. I had been in the advanced classes when I dropped out. We stayed together for a few years, but when he came back from Korea four years later, he was a drug addict. The soldiers had lots of drugs and when he came back addicted to heroin, domestic violence set in. There were two terrible incidents. I heard about a man who killed his daughter's abuser and went to jail. I couldn't tell my dad and brothers or they would have killed him. My husband stole and sold the children's clothes. When he told me I had to prostitute my body for money for his drugs, I knew I had to leave; I took my two little ones and got on a Greyhound bus to California. They were 6 and 7 years old and the trip across the country took 2 and half days.

Who or what was in California?

NR: A childhood friend, one of the boys in that group picture on the wall, was in the Navy and he knew about the violence; he said if I ever came to California he would help me get on my feet and take care of the kids. We were compatible. We lived together, but lo and behold he turned out to be an alcoholic. He worked well during the day but drank and drank in the evening. He was what's called a functional alcoholic. So I was in two bad situations in my life. A friend in California produced a documentary about my story for her master's thesis in film editing. This documentary won first place at Rutgers University during Women's History Month. Groups around the country are using it as a teaching tool.

Where did you live in California?

NR: When the bus pulled in at the Los Angeles bus terminal, I thought oh no! My first impression of California was that it looked just the same as the bus terminal in New York City. My heart just sank. It was the same sort of place. However, we first lived in Perris, which is now Moreno Valley, and then we moved to Compton for a short while. After that, most of my years in California were spent in Pomona and Orange County. I was 24, with two small children when I took the long distance trip on the Greyhound bus. I feel that every life experience has been a blessing. Even the bad times made me stronger. My first real job in California was at Buffam's Department Store, which was like a Neiman Marcus. I was a sales clerk in the book department on the first floor right by the entrance door, and that's when I got my first taste of racism.

You didn't face racism in Brooklyn?

NR: Oh no! We grew up with Irish, Jewish and Polish--all kinds of ethnic people. I didn't know what racism was in New York City. Never. In fact I had a friend in public school with me, who had recently moved to New York from the south; when we first took the bus together to Washington Irving School, she wanted to sit at the back of the bus. I said, "Why are you sitting at the back?" She said, "They allow us to sit at the front?" This was the early 50s. I didn't know about that kind of racism. But years later in California, I had customers at the department store, especially women, who wouldn't put money in my hand. They put their money on the counter. A few went up to the manager's station to file a complaint, saying, "Why do you have an African American working on the first floor?" I was the only minority on the first floor, another female minority worked on the second floor. We were the only two in the whole store.

So, then did they transfer you?

NR: Nope. They later made me the manager! I knew how to sell books. Do you know what it was like working in a bookstore? I walked into my library every day! I was surrounded by knowledge. From there I went to work for Walden Books as a manager. I was the first minority manager at Walden Books.

How did you get such a great job?

NR: A good friend who was German and I were working together at a computer place when a friend of hers told her about the job at Buffam's. She was hired and she told me. Through her I got the job and we worked together. When she left to manage at one Walden Books, she got me the job at another store. That's when I discovered myself. I learned how to drive when I was 40 years old. I read everything I could put my hands on. Freud, Jung, Gestalt therapy, Ayn Rand. I just ate it all up and I came to realize that in my relationships I was the enabler. I was allowing what was happening. I wasn't taking the steps to make changes. When my marriage became impossible because of the domestic violence, I left. But I stayed almost 11 years in the second relationship. His alcoholism happened gradually. I never married him. I never got a divorce either. I never saw my husband again after I fled from New York, but I about a year ago I learned that he died in 1998.

So he never asked for a divorce either?

NR: No. I started to get a divorce, filled out all the paper work myself, and yet for some reason didn't follow through. Yet, one of the most important aspects of my personality was to learn how to forgive. To this day, every time I visit my youngest daughter in California, I visit her father who is now in an assisted living place. He is partially paralyzed, in a wheel chair. We are cordial and we are able to share present experiences. Forgiveness is a treasured virtue.

Years ago you told me that your parents were against your marriage because his skin was too dark and that they wanted to "lighten "the family.

NR: That's true. I was a kid, and I didn't realize that they were prejudiced until I wanted to marry this very dark skinned man. The only reason they allowed it was because I was pregnant. But they worshipped my children. Years later my daughter lived in New York and took care of my mom and dad. Strangely enough, my brother married an African American, although she's pretty light skinned. My other brother also married an African American. So I was a pioneer.

But looking at that photo of your parents, they aren't light skinned.

NR: No, they were not, but my mother had a sister with red hair and freckles. Ah, something landed in Puerto Rico. Let's get back to not graduating. I told myself one day I'm going back to school. I did go to early adult education in California and opened a daycare in our church. That opened the door for me. That adult education made me realize I wanted an education. So I got my GED in 1980. Then I moved here to help my oldest daughter who was in the Air Force with her baby son who is now in medical school in the military. He's happily married with two children now. Anyway, I moved to San Antonio in 1986 and it took eleven years before I enrolled in St. Philip's in 1997. During that time period I took care of my grandson and my parents who relocated from Brooklyn. They were well on in years and it was a blessing for me to honor them with tender loving care. Once they arrived, I quit my little job working at a daycare center. After nine years my dad passed away in 1994; then my mom said, "You are going to college and get your degree. You are going to get your degree. You've waited long enough to accomplish your heart's desire."

And you were the valedictorian when you graduated from St. Philips!

NR: Yes! And I dedicated my speech to my mom. Much to my surprise, my speech was aired on NPR for a whole month!

How many children do you have, Nereida?

NR: Three. My son Louis Ralph better known as Poncho is 62, and a daughter Pauline known as Cookie who is 61 are from my marriage. They were on the Greyhound bus to California with me. I also have one daughter from the second relationship, Jenev Adrianne. When I was a struggling young mother, I never would have imagined that in the winter of my years my children would become my best friends. It's a wonderful feeling knowing one is secure and happy when sharing a life with one's children until death do us part.

How old were you when you went back to school at UTSA?

NR: I was 67 when I received my associate's degree and 72 when I got my bachelor's at UTSA. I waited and dreamt for 45 years. It was a joy. And, it's a joy to be an English tutor now at St. Philip's. I work there three days a week. They wanted me to teach some classes years ago, but I said, "I'm 72! And I don't want to bring home essays to grade. I want to come home and be free. I see what the teachers go through. No, no, no!" I pick my hours and pick my days, yet I'm always willing to fill in the gap when needed. I love my job, encouraging students is a passion.

Did you contemplate going on and getting a master's degree?

NR: I took all the required courses but I did not pass the MA exam. The test requires specific recall of about forty different works of literature from different periods. My memory wasn't up to it. Bonnie told me I could take the exam again. I considered that option briefly but then I thought about Chaucer and Patient Griselda and when Griselda's husband said, "Enough is enough, Griselda!" That's what I thought. It was such a relief. I completed the whole program but didn't retake the MA exam.

But for you the goal was to learn not get a degree anyhow.

NR: That's so true. In my graduation speech at St. Philip's, I said, "I never had a chance to wear a prom dress. I never had a chance to wear a wedding gown. But now is my chance. I'm wearing a cap and gown." I graduated cum laude. I was in honors classes. I even earned a scholarship to take a trip to Puerto Rico in order to do research for my bachelor's thesis.

Have you published any of your stories?

NR: No. There they are sitting right there on the shelf. I hope that one day I'll take the giant step and submit them for publication. This way I have something to look forward to. I learned so much and changed so much throughout my years. Each day allows me a new and grand experience. I never have found my life boring, and I keep a personal journal. And my children bring me so much joy.

It sounds like you motivated your kids.

NR: My children are fabulous even though we all suffered through tough times. I have 9 grandchildren and 6 great grands.

When you won that trip to Puerto Rico, was that your first trip there?

NR: Oh, no. My cousin lives there and I'd been many times. My mom never wanted to go back because she grew up in such miserable poverty, but my dad went back and forth. In 2000 my cousin Gloria and I took a 7-week trip to Europe. It was her treat after she retired. We visited Greece, Italy, Paris and Germany. I also visit my grands and great grandchildren in California yearly.

Did you have a favorite place?

NR: Florence. I was crazy for Florence. I spent three solid hours at Dante Alighieri's home, which was turned into a museum. I had studied his life in one of my honors classes. I've also gone to Belize and visited a brother who lives in Aruba. I love to travel, cook, swim, and read good books.

What are you reading now?

NR: I'm reading the "Left Behind" series and just finished "Buffalo Girls" by Larry McMurtry. It's about the prostitutes and old timers in the Old West and about how the west was changing and modernizing. It's a wonderful story about when out goes the old and in comes the new. I'm always reading. I also read the recently published Harper Lee's "Go Set a Watchman." It's quite a complex novel with a few surprises. You know "Huck Finn" was the first book I read that had the word nigger in it. We never heard that word in Brooklyn. As I said, my first brush with racism was in California in the middle of white flight. This was when white families wanted to get away as black people moved into their neighborhoods. Interracial marriages were their greatest fear. When I lived in Pomona the school system wanted to bus my children to elementary school. I didn't drive and I didn't want my kids far away from me, so I refused to let them be bused.

It doesn't sound like racism ever held you back.

NR: Never. Never! Picture this at Walden Books in Beverly Hills at an autograph party: Everyone in the room is white. Everyone. Then the black maids come out with their little black skirts and traditional maids' uniforms handing out hors d'oeuvres and I'm sitting there a manager earning a decent wage doing something I loved. For that, I thank God.

So, even though California was the first time you witnessed racism it never affected you.

NR: I was hired because of my girlfriend. All of my early jobs were because of her. I've never had a resume. When I moved here and applied at the daycare center they hired me because of my experience at Friendship Infant and Day Care at my church in California. At St. Philip's when I was asked me to be a tutor at the Rose R. Thomas Writing center, I didn't even want to work. I wanted to concentrate on my own studies. I was already helping other students with their essays, and because the Writing Center was reopening in 1999 they were desperate for tutors. I just had to fill out the necessary paperwork but there was no resume or interview. And, I've been tutoring at St. Philip's ever since. As the result of my position as a tutor, I am able to remain financially independent to this day.

That's extraordinary.

NR: God is good. I was born again in 1976. I've been attending Leon Valley Baptist Church since 1987. I am very active and throughout the years have been involved in developing various ministries. In fact I took two years off from tutoring from 2008-2010 in order to teach second grade at the Christian Academy at my church. It was a wonderful experience. What is also important to me is when I am able to help students from foreign countries with their essays. We can talk about different faiths, customs, and food. I especially enjoy talking to the young students from Saudi Arabia and a few of them call me mama.

It's your dazzling smile and upbeat personality. They love you, of course!

NR: Yes, but sometimes I think it's because I can cook!

What do you cook?

NR: Puerto Rican dishes. I don't eat out much because I cook better than most restaurants! I pray over my pots when I cook!

What will you have tonight?

NR: Black rice and baked pork smothered with onions and peppers. I also make *arroz con pollo* (red rice with chicken) which is accompanied with *habichuela* (beans). My signature dish is *penil* (roast pork shoulder).

What music do you like?

NR: All kinds, especially smooth jazz and gospel. I have tickets to see Yanni at the Majestic. My daughter who doesn't live in San Antonio is flying in from California and we'll have dinner on the Riverwalk and then go to the concert. It will be a unique evening for mother and both daughters.

Do your friends live in this retirement community?

NR: No, most of my neighbors stay home. We are friendly as neighbors, but most of my friends are younger, and I know them from church or the writing center. My life has been good. And I had no plan. The only thing I knew for sure was that I didn't want another relationship with a man. I didn't want the complication. I didn't want anyone to ask me to cook dinner or iron shirts. I wanted to find myself. I've even written a short story about self-discovery in a creative writing class.

Do you have a hard time making women friends because of your independent attitude?

NR: Not really. Once they know me, they don't feel threatened. And, I'm interested and curious about people even if they are different. I get along with almost anyone. Knowing that life is short, my wisest investment has been investing in others. I think I am a pretty good listener, which is an acquired skill; therefore talking with others is a joy. What breaks my heart is knowing that there are elderly people who have no one to share their concerns and joys with. Okay, now I have a treat for us. Excuse me while I go boil some water for tea.

It's lovely sitting here by your window and enjoying the breeze. Isn't it nice to finally be able to have the windows open?

NR: My windows! I love them! I can spend hours looking out of my windows. I chose this unit specifically for the location and windows. My neighbors ask if I'm not worried I'll get killed in a drive-by shooting. I say, ya gotta go somehow. They just gave us screen doors last spring so I leave my door open until it gets dark and enjoy a double breeze. I enjoy my little place.

Hey, you have a tattoo on your wrist!

NR: Yes, I got it for my fiftieth birthday from my daughters. We were spending time together at Laguna Beach and I couldn't think of a grander birthday gift.

How did you choose the spot on your body?

NR: I wanted the tattoo to be where everyone could see it. It's a sea horse. I collect them as memorabilia. It's the male that carries the eggs in his pouch until they are ready to be laid. Being ready in life is so important for creative development. That reminds me of Langston Hughes's poem about a dream deferred. Dreams do come true in time and with God's help I have come a long way from a victim of domestic violence and dependence. And I will be ready for my final rest.

Algebra

by Nereida Reyes

It's far beyond my comprehension why algebra deserves attention.

Letters, numbers everywhere, some are here and some are there.

You add, subtract, you multiply and then here comes my great divide.

I sit and wonder how it can be; letter, numbers play in infinity.

Then I try to play with them and figure what they mean.

It doesn't work; I just get lost somewhere in space or in-between.

But in my dreams and pillow soft, I tell these figures I'm the boss!

I try and try and try again, but all I do is fret and toss.

I see square 2, hear exponent X, both keeping me quite perplexed.

But I'm determined I will win, and when I'm through I sure will sing.

I'll jump and whoop and holler high I'll play with them in their own sky.

For never in my wildest dreams did I plan algebra in my dreams.

Marga Speicher was born in Germany in 1934; surviving World War II was her childhood. Coming to Texas with a religious order, which she left several years later, she initially worked as a social worker but later found her real calling as a psychologist. She still has clients and lectures frequently, particularly about interpreting images and metaphors from dreams, literature, and fairytales.

MARGA SPEICHER

We've looked forward to this interview because what little we know of you is that you've had a very different and interesting life.

MS: Well, I've had a life full of twists and turns. There is an old Chinese saying: May you live in interesting times.

That saying is a curse, isn't it?

MS: Yes, it is a curse. In hindsight we can also call the times "interesting." A lot of experiences and events we live through are stepping-stones and lead us forward. Some are funny years later, but at the time they are neither funny nor interesting. That's a big piece of my life.

So, what are the twists and turns of your life? Let's start at the beginning. Where were you born? Where and how did you grow up?

MS: I was born in 1934 in the Saar District of Germany, near the French border. My father came from a rural area. His father was a baker and local postmaster; most of my father's siblings were coalminers and worked in the fields, raising crops for their use. He was the "smart kid" who went further in school, entered civil service and obtained a position in the city where he was an administrator in the finance section of the local courthouse. My mother's family owned and operated a small grocery and general merchandise store in a steel mill city of 35,000 inhabitants, Voelklingen. Everyone in the family worked in the store and the boys pursued higher education. My mother wanted to become a teacher but lived in an era and family where '"the boys go to school and the girls get married." She was very unhappy about not having been able to become a teacher. She valued education and was a force for education for her children. My parents' early years as a couple were quite traditional and harmonious. Then the war upended everything-- rumors of war in 1938; war itself in 1939. World War II strongly impacted our family and my life as it did everyone alive at the time. Because we lived near the border with France, we were evacuated in September 1939 before the German invasion of France when Germany cleared the area of civilians – and then again in September 1944 when the German military intended to make a last stand of defense in the border area and cleared it of civilians again. As "evacuees" we lived in central Germany where we were assigned; we carried only the few belongings we were allowed to take with us.

Did your father serve in the German Army?

My father was drafted into the Army in 1939 like every able-bodied male; he came home for two weeks of annual leave throughout the war. He was home for one year, '41-'42, on an "Essential for Civilian Service" exemption. He was on the Eastern front throughout the war and in the final battle east of Berlin in 1945. He was "missing in action" for several years after the war; we hoped so strongly for his return but hope subsided over time. In 1953 we received a definitive answer: a large mass grave had been found where his military ID tag was located. During the war, my mother received regular letters and we children received an occasional postcard, real treasures. In 1943, my father, unexpectedly, came home on leave on Christmas day and brought a live duck as a present for us children: he had bartered with a farmer in the Crimea, giving away his cigarette rations for the duck he carried home during an arduous trip with multiple train rides.

What are your memories of those war years?

MS: I lived through many nights in air raid shelters; I was well aware of combat, war, destruction; I remember vividly the day when the American Army captured the village in central Germany where we were living as evacuees. I remember the winter of 1944-45, when it was clear to all (including us 10-year old fourth-grade girls) that either the Allied Army or the Russian Army would capture the village. Being very afraid of Russians who had a reputation of raping girls and women, we 10-year old girls prayed that the American Army would get to us before the Russians.

What were the post-war years like?

The post-war years of 1945-47 were years of much struggle for obtaining basic goods for survival: food was in short supply; in '45-'46, there was not much to buy even if one had rationing cards and money. Bartering was the order of the day. City folk searched closets for anything that could be bartered (clothing, children's toys, extra dishes, etc.) for food when farmers came to town with their products. My mother was ingenious and creative in finding ways — we pulled together and did okay. We lived very simply, in small quarters (our apartment in my parents' house had been confiscated by the occupation forces) but we had our own place and we were never hungry.

How were your school experiences affected?

MS: My early years in school were marked, on the one hand, by Nazi indoctrination, and, on the other hand, by family values and standards that were quite different. I learned to never tell anyone outside our home what was being said inside the home. I was not allowed to take part in government-sponsored school activities unless they were obligatory. I could not understand why I could not go to something like "story hour" or crafts activities with the other children. I remember one time I walked into the kitchen and saw my grandfather standing on a chair with his ear against the radio that was high on the top shelf. When he saw me, he turned off the radio and told me he was trying to fix the radio. I think now that he was listening to a foreign sender, which was illegal. Children were told in school what was permitted and what was not and were encouraged to tell about what their families were saying and doing; in adult language: to inform on their families. Such information put families at risk of being interrogated and possibly jailed. You never let anybody know anything. I was smart enough to know not to tell anyone what happened in my home. Gestapo (the Secret Police) were ever-present.

What about your religious life?

MS: My family were practicing Catholics--and religious practice was forbidden by the state. In particular, it was illegal for churches to hold religious instruction classes: the state wanted to educate the youth through the state's youth movement in state ideologies. My parents sent me and my brother to religious instruction classes held in secret at church. In the smaller communities like our small town, some activities were possible if low key enough; in the metropolitan areas, Nazi oppression was much stronger. I remember seeing strange men in the back of our church writing notes in little books. After the war, I learned that they were Gestapo or at least sympathizers who wrote down the names of the men who went to church. In 1942, my father lost his exemption from military service ("Essential for Civilian Service" category) because he had gone to church and he was sending his children to church. My father was in the military; he had never been a Nazi party member, although there had been pressure on him to join. My mother told me that in later years.

Tell us about the post-war years.

MS: For me and my classmates and, probably, for my generation in general, the post-war years were marked by four things: First, engagement with the *events of the war years*; of dictatorship; of war and destruction; of anti-Semitism and the Holocaust; of German responsibility and guilt, individual and collective. On the one hand, all of the 1945 German textbooks, created by the Allied Command, contained Holocaust history and Holocaust survivor stories in great detail. Our "reading texts" contained almost exclusively Holocaust stories. On the other hand, in history classes in later years, we somehow never completed a history textbook: the semester ended by the time we reached the chapters around 1914. We did not get to the years after that. Second, exploration of the *multiple factors that led to the Hitler totalitarian regime*, to Holocaust and all-out war. I began such exploration during my teen years. It intensified into a major, internal confrontation in my 30s, when I was already in the US; it has been and will remain ongoing. Third, a sparking of youthful idealism and fervor into 'No More War' activities. I remember writing an essay in the late 40s: entitled "Why we need a United Europe, "I remember being active in the youth movement for intercultural exchange between the former enemies: Germany and France; I remember being vociferous in school about the movement toward establishing the beginnings of what would become the European Union. My first professional interest was to become an interpreter and work for the European Union. Later, that interest morphed into following in the footsteps of Albert Schweitzer, into becoming a physician in underserved areas of the world. Fourth, I developed strong feelings against authoritarian, dictatorial stances – initially focused on politics but then extending across a range of spheres of life. One might say that I have an allergic reaction to anything that looks dictatorial to me!

Did anything else emerge in your post-war years?

MS: The school years fostered my love for reading. In my mid-teens, I found more insight in literature than in history books. Several figures and themes emerged out of my reading and stayed with me; they became lights for the way and increasingly meaningful. To this day, they continue to lead to new perspectives. For example, Sophocles' play "Antigone" deeply affected me. When Antigone decides to bury her traitorous brother even if it costs her life, she says, "*Nicht mitzuhassen, mitzulieben bin ich da. – I do not exist to hate. I exist to love.*" That speaks to me—and for me.

Can you tell us more about your own worldview and the influence of the arts?

MS: The influence of the arts on creating one's worldview, on psychological development, has been a major area of interest for me. I wrote my 'Final Paper' at the end of psychoanalytic training in 1983 on that topic and two years later enlarged it into my doctoral thesis. In the process of working on those papers, I re-read most of the writing that I had been significant for me. For example, in rereading Antoine de St. Expiry's *The Little Prince*, I remembered being struck by his devotion to caring for and protecting his flower. In 1982-83, however, I was struck by the question of what in me needed the protection and caring devotion I saw in the little prince.

In addition to literature what do you take with you from those years?

M: In recent years, I have wondered about the influence of the geography and history of the Saar District; they have become metaphors for themes in my life. The Saar District lies on the boundary between Germany and France and the image of 'boundary' has become meaningful to me. Boundaries require that we see each other, that we see "other" as well as "self," that we find ways to see each other and get to know each other without losing oneself and without rejecting the other. All life is lived on some boundary – how we respond to that reality becomes one of life's tasks.

Tell us more, please, about your life after the war.

MS: When I was 20, in January 1955, I joined a Catholic religious community called *Schoenstatt Sisters of Mary* with an aim of devoting my life to service to others in a contemporary mode. While functioning very similarly to a Catholic religious order, the community had a different, more contemporary structure, called 'secular institute' in Catholic Church law vs. 'congregation' or 'order.' Potential members have a period of formation, then make a temporary 'contract' (vs. vows), then a lifetime contract. The structure of the community is more contemporary; their fields of service were wide reaching; there was more inclusion of individual interests than in other orders at that time. I volunteered for overseas assignment and was assigned to the United States. In 1956, I came to Corpus Christi, where the Sisters worked for the diocese, mostly in parish work. For one year, I worked in a kindergarten in a parochial school. It became clear quite quickly that teaching small children was not my calling! In 1957, the diocese of Corpus Christi was considering the establishment of a Catholic Welfare Bureau and was looking to have someone obtain professional education in social work to lead a social service agency for the diocese. I had an interest in such work and started graduate school in social work in fall 1957 at the Worden School of Social

Service at what is now Our Lady of the Lake University in San Antonio and lived in the dormitory. The two-year program was intensive and immersed me in the experience and understanding of personal, family, and community problems along with diverse means of approaching potential solutions. When I graduated in 1959, however, the diocese of Corpus Christi had other priorities, and I ended up working in the Catholic Welfare Bureau (CWB) in San Antonio. Since the community to which I belonged did not have a local group and house here, I lived in a residence staffed by another group but went monthly to my community's house in Corpus Christi. I worked at CWB until 1962 when there was a shift in direction for CWB, and several professional staff positions were eliminated. Quickly, we "eliminated ones" obtained positions in other San Antonio family service agencies. Later, I worked in the outpatient clinic at San Antonio State Hospital, a move that marked a major change of direction into the mental health field, a shift that awakened my potential and evoked "my calling" to professional development in psychodynamic, in-depth psychotherapy. I took additional graduate studies in psychology (leading to the MA in Psychology); training in psychotherapy and psychoanalysis with a focus on the work of C.G. Jung (leading to the diploma as Jungian Psychoanalyst); doctoral study in psychoanalytic theories (leading to the Ph.D. in Psychoanalytic Studies). After the late seventies, I worked full-time as a psychotherapist and psychoanalyst and have had a satisfying professional life working with clients, teaching young professionals, and participating in professional organizations.

What were the major developments in your personal life?

MS: Yes, let's get back there! During the years of "temporary contract'" in the religious community, I was in turmoil about whether this was my vocation or not. There was nothing concrete or specific that troubled me although I found living in a hierarchical structure constricting. Over time, after much internal struggle and reflection, I realized that my vocation was not life-long commitment to living in a structured, religious community. In late 1962, I sought release from the contract and left the community in February 1963. When I left, I received a sum of money to tide me over into civilian life. Most importantly, I had a professional education, a job, and friends. I had a life here, so the transition to civilian life was eased in general although the financial transition was difficult. For instance, my paychecks had always gone to the community that paid for fixed expenses and supplied a certain amount for incidental expenses. But, now, setting up living on my own, I had a hard time getting an apartment and a car since I had no credit rating.

Was it spiritually troubling to leave the order? It always seems to me that people who make a religious commitment have answers and if you give that up, you join the rest of us who have only questions.

MS: I think that there is a process for everyone away from '"having answers" to "living with the questions" and then, even later, to "living the questions." When I was 18, I knew absolutely what was right and wrong, but, after that age of certainty, I gradually "knew" less and less and I surely ended up having only questions and uncertainties. I already had questions when I made my second contract but I was not yet ready to make a decision to leave. The actual "leaving'" was the endpoint of an extended process of maturation.

How did your family respond?

MS: My mother was shocked and hurt, mostly because I did not return to Germany. She came to visit and was convinced I would return with her and was even more hurt when I did not. I had become an American citizen during the years in the community, and my intention was to stay in this country. In hindsight I will say that I had become emotionally, psychologically, intellectually an adult in the United States; my life was here, and the thought of returning to Germany did not really occur to me in a serious way. It had not been my mother's wish that I join the community. She never wanted me to do that. I had joined the community against her wishes and I stayed in the United States against her wishes.

Are you still a Catholic?

MS: No. I remained a Catholic for several years after 1963 but I moved away from all organized religion over a period of time. Now, I have a spiritual attitude without adhering to any creed or specific religious tradition. My husband was Jewish, and he was a member of a local synagogue. I still maintain connections and relationships with that congregation as a friend, but I am not a member.

Have you lived in San Antonio for many years now?

MS: After I left the community I stayed in San Antonio and lived and worked here; I dated some, fostered my friendships and adjusted to life outside an organized community. In 1969, I started to work in the establishment of the mental health clinic for the Department of Psychiatry at the medical school that had recently opened. That move led to another turning point for me. The medical school recruited many mental health professionals from all over the country. Prior to that time, I was a big fish in a tiny pond, but I then recognized that the pond was getting bigger, and I realized I did not have the education and training I needed in order to be on equal footing with my peers. So, I explored additional educational opportunities. I realized that New York City offered a vast range of opportunities, and I decided to move there and then figure out specific plans. I sold most of my possessions, packed what was left into my car, and drove to NYC when I was 37. I found an apartment and got a job in a clinic where I worked for two years. In fall 1973, I started taking classes at the New School for Social Research, which had open admissions if your credentials were acceptable. The MSW from Worden School at OLLU served as my basis for admission and I obtained an MA in Personality Theory. I always say that The New School is where I learned to think. To further develop clinical skills, I decided to seek psychoanalytic training. C.G. Jung's thinking had always appealed to me and I became engaged in an intensive, 6-year program at the C.G. Jung Institute in NY. That is where I became a good therapist. Later, I received a doctoral degree in Psychoanalysis from Union College. Throughout all those years of ongoing education, I continued to work full-time

So you have two master's degrees and a PhD?

MS: Yes. In my view, more important than the academic and clinical study was the personal growth through immersion in an in-depth process of personal psychotherapy. I had become aware that many distressing experiences from my early life were affecting me negatively and needed exploration and working through; I had sought psychotherapy before entering the analytic program and continued it throughout. Personal therapy is a requirement in psychoanalytic training programs. It is the process of in-depth psychotherapy through which I became the fuller human being that I have become as well as the psychotherapist I aim to be. Without that process, I would not be who and what I am. This personal process once again connected me deeply with the world of images that had been so meaningful to me in the literary tradition and that now opened to me more strongly, leading to images becoming guideposts to inner dynamics: images in dreams and in the metaphors of literature, folklore, events of everyday life. That process led to exploration of folklore, to teaching and leading workshops for professionals and for the general public on opening the world of metaphor across a wide range of experiences.

When and how did you meet your husband?

MS: I met my husband in New York City in 1978. He was in the financial services industry and had moved to NYC after his divorce in 1977. He was twelve years older than I and had traveled extensively in his work.

His world sounds very different from yours, how did you meet him?

M: Through a mutual friend who thought we had some things in common and who said: "Even if there is not romance, you might become friends." To begin with, we enjoyed bike riding. On our first date we rode all the way from uptown to the Battery and took the ferry to Staten Island. On the ferry he asked if I intended to invite him up to my apartment when we returned. The next day and the rest of that week, on his evening bike ride, he somehow ended up in my neighborhood and called, wondering whether he could come up to the apartment for a visit. We enjoyed each other's company and felt compatible although we were very different. We started living together fairly soon and we were married three years later.

Was he your first lover?

M: He was my first real lover but I had had romantic and sexual relationships before. I also had a relationship with a man where there was one-sided love (mine) and where my heart was broken. Neither my husband nor I ever proposed marriage; our relationship simply evolved toward marriage. In fact, early in the relationship, he had told me "I will never get married again. If you want marriage, do not go out with me." After we had been together about 2½ years, he came home one night and said: "I had the weirdest thought on the bus coming home: we should get married." I simply said, "Sure, when do we do it? "

What brought you back to San Antonio?

M: We were married in September 1981. Over time, NYC became increasingly expensive and in the early '90s we started to talk about where we wanted to grow old together. We did not want to ever move to a retirement community, and we did not think we were rich enough to grow old in or around NYC. Very deliberately we decided to look for a location with a lower cost of living, a city that was large enough so that I could still work and that had a cultural life. Most of all, it had to be south of New York; I did not want to grow old having to navigate ice and snow for months! I suggested San Antonio; I still had friends and colleagues here. We came to visit and browsed around, and I reconnected with some people. We decided San Antonio made the most sense as a place for us to live. We knew what we wanted and were pragmatic about finances. We moved here in 1994.

Are you still working?

MS: I am still working, part-time. I no longer accept new patients; I still see people with whom I have worked for some time. I occasionally teach workshops and give lectures.

For many women the major decision of their life has been getting married. For you, was it leaving the order?

M: I do not consider that step as the most significant one but as <u>one</u> major influence; there were others. Joining the religious community was a significant step; growing out of it was another. Another major point was personal psychotherapy to work through my non-resolved emotional dilemmas and conflicts so that I could become my own person in a solid way. Then, there was realization that I needed more intellectual stimulation. Leaving San Antonio to go to NYC was a major step. Meeting my husband was another major point. Ours was a late-in-life true love relationship between two mature people. We gave each other truly unconditional love, acceptance, and respect. However, that does not mean we never had disagreements; we did have plenty of those. But we had a solid foundation in a warm, giving relationship with much sharing.

Do you look back much?

MS: Oh yes. I do look in the rear view mirror. I ask myself: what if I had done this or that? Usually when I look back, I see what I might have had but then I also see what I would not have had. At present, looking back leads more to seeing good outcomes than to seeing the troubles it took to get there – although I am aware of the troubles of the road. And I am deeply grateful for all the gifts that life has given me.

Do you have any major regrets?

MS: Surely. One of my big wishes was/is that I had fallen in love and had a lasting relationship in my thirties so I could have had children. I always wanted children. But I had cervical cancer and a hysterectomy in my late thirties and having children was then no longer possible. I feel very fortunate that both of my husband's daughters and their children are close to me. Oh, let me tell you about a very sweet experience: one of the Leon's daughters called, during her first pregnancy, to tell me that she and her husband had decided that in our family there would be no step-grandparents. She told me that I had been important in her life and that I would be a "full and real grandmother.'" I'm very delighted in that role. Now: would I want not to have my relationship with these two women and their families and with my grandchildren? NO. I would not want to give up those relationships!

Did your mother ever meet your husband?

M: Yes, we went to Germany together and she was very friendly to him and accepting even though she did not like the idea that I had married here. She wanted me to return to Germany.

Why didn't you want to return?

MS: I had my life here. Deep down, I think I also needed to be away from my mother's influence. She was so bereft after my father's death that the situation could have become one where the daughter gets drafted into the position of taking care of the mother (of becoming the "emotional spouse") when the father does not return from the war. It is part of the old tradition. I think, intuitively, I knew I did not want that. By the time I left the religious community I was becoming my own person and was carving my own life. I wanted my own life and it was here.

It seems that the focus of your earlier life was on learning and education. Is that true?

MS: No, not fully. My life overall has been about service. Education and work were parts of that larger process. The degrees were tools; I pursued the training and the degrees because I knew that in order to provide better service I needed to do so.

So you maintained the attitudes about service that led you to enter the religious community even when you left it?

MS: I always wanted to be of service. I spoke earlier about Sophocles' "Antigone." One might say that Antigone is my saint. Her statement "I do not exist to hate. I exist to love" is a guidepost. Joining the religious community was my way to channel my life into service. If the Peace Corps had existed in Germany at that time, I might have taken that route. Leaving the community was for the same reason. I felt I needed a broader arena.

What is your life like these days?

MS: Since I am mostly retired, I have become a subscriber to slow living. It is important to me to take time, to live, to be. This morning I read Amy Lowell's poem "Leisure" and it expressed so much of what is now important to me: "That sole condition of all loveliness, The dreaming lapse of slow, unmeasured time." In the 'Prologue' to Demian, Hermann Hesse, says, "I have been a seeker and remain one . . . each person's life is a road to oneself, the attempt to a way, the pointing to a path." The narrative of my life is "an attempt to a way, the pointing to a path." My life has been lived in two languages and two cultural spheres: German and English: the cultural and philosophical traditions and thinking of the German-European and US-American spheres. I have lived in each and between them. As I have become older, the significance of the early cultural influences has come to the surface more strongly. In my early years in the US, there were times when I experienced major conflicts in cultural, ethnic, religious traditions and in their impact on personal identity. I no longer experience those differences as conflicts; I now can say that I come out of a German cultural and Catholic religious tradition; therein lie my roots. Over time, layers of experiences and of new awareness and knowledge of diverse traditions and perspectives have been added. It is possible to come to live in multiplicities without being torn by them. Life is cumulative; experiences on multiple levels enrich and deepen us. Looking back on why I remained in the US without even considering returning to Germany, I now think that, at that time, the differences between my German self and my American self were in serious conflict. Remaining in the US was my way, at the time, of side-stepping the conflict and fundamentally siding with my emerging adulthood. The "solution" at that moment precluded consideration of leaving that sphere. At the time, I was not aware of that underlying dynamic and surely could not have articulated it.

AFTERWORD

What I, Deb Field, love most about this collection of interviews is that despite how different the women and their lives are a consistent thread of optimism and fortitude prevails in each story. All of these women chose to focus on life and the goodness that was and is available. They focused on potential rather than roadblocks. They looked forward and positively propelled themselves rather than getting slogged down by their obstacles. Their momentum continues into their 80s and 90s. They still project their gaze on the future and what is possible. Most of these women had serious limits put on their lives, but they stepped over the lines and dared to challenge the norm and themselves.

Life isn't the straight line I thought it was when I was younger. We go from point A to point B and so on but the line is curved and often jagged. Many of us learn that it's been in the detours and roadblocks that our life has taken on depth and meaning. The unpredictable and unimaginable can be the most significant markers in our lives. It's fascinating to listen to how the women in this book got from where they began to where they are now physically, spiritually, intellectually, and emotionally.

A long time ago a wise person told me that the secret to life is to live with joy and grace. Sounds easy, doesn't it? I'm not saying that these women are models of perfection and have found the magical key to the kingdom of happiness, but they have figured things out in a way that has allowed them to walk through their days with an abundance of grace and joy.

Since I was in my 30s I've had friends who were a decade or more older than I. Most are now in their 70s and some in their 80s. They defy all the clichés. They live alone, go to the gym, have active social lives, participate in community affairs, drive and do all the things a person does. Many still work and either teach or take classes.

In a world that is dominated by the glorification of youth, especially for women, it is time to realize the benefits of age and recognize the accomplishments of lives well lived. A life well lived. What is that? None of the women we interviewed invented penicillin or won a Noble Prize. Instead they lived extraordinary, normal lives. They had and still have wit, gumption, humor, courage and fortitude. Their stories are remarkable because of who they are, not what they did. They remind me that when I inventory my life not to pay attention to what I did or what happened to me but to value who I am and how I have behaved. Our life itineraries and timelines are merely reference points. All of these women are interesting and have lived interesting lives because they have been interested. Their vitality and curiosity propelled and still propel them.

CPSIA information can be obtained
at www.ICGtesting.com
Printed in the USA
LVOW09s2153310517
536512LV00007B/356/P

9 781478 783145